# Moments of our nights and days

## Also by Ruth Burgess:

*Candles and Conifers: Resources for All Saints' and Advent*

*Hay and Stardust: Resources from Christmas to Candlemas*

*Eggs and Ashes: Practical and liturgical resources for Lent and Holy Week*

*Fire and Bread: Resources from Easter Day to Trinity Sunday*

*Bare Feet and Buttercups: Resources for Ordinary Time – Trinity Sunday to the Feast of the Transfiguration*

*Acorns and Archangels: Resources for Ordinary Time – The Feast of the Transfiguration to All Hallows'*

*Saying Goodbye: Resources for funerals, scattering ashes and remembering*

*Friends and Enemies: A book of short prayers & some ways to write your own*

*A Book of Blessings ... and how to write your own*

*Hear My Cry: A daily prayer book for Advent*

*Praying for the Dawn: A resource book for the ministry of healing* (with Kathy Galloway)

All published by Wild Goose Publications

# Moments of
# our nights and days

Liturgies and resources for baptisms, weddings,
partnerships, friendships and the journey of life

## Ruth Burgess

**wild goose
publications**

www.**ionabooks**.com

First published 2014 by
Wild Goose Publications, Fourth Floor, Savoy House,
140 Sauchiehall Street, Glasgow G2 3DH, UK,
the publishing division of the Iona Community.
Scottish Charity No. SC003794. Limited Company Reg. No. SC096243.

ISBN 978-1-84952-309-7

Cover photograph © Ruth Burgess

The publishers gratefully acknowledge the support of the Drummond Trust, 3 Pitt Terrace,
Stirling FK8 2EY in producing this book.

Overseas distribution
Australia: Willow Connection Pty Ltd, Unit 4A, 3–9 Kenneth Road, Manly Vale, NSW 2093
New Zealand: Pleroma, Higginson Street, Otane 4170, Central Hawkes Bay
Canada: Bayard Distribution, 10 Lower Spadina Ave., Suite 400, Toronto, Ontario M5V 2Z

Printed by Bell & Bain, Thornliebank, Glasgow

# Contents

# Contents in detail

### Key to symbols

| | |
|---|---|
| ✞ | Prayer |
| ☒ | Liturgy |
| ((○)) | Responsive prayer |
| ♫ | Song/Music |
| ✿ | Reflective prayer |
| ⊞ | Reflection |
| ✶ | Poem |
| ✍ | Story |
| ↩ | Reading |
| ⚲ | Practical |

## Bits and pieces for baptisms, dedications, blessings and naming ceremonies    71

## Liturgies of baptism for older children and adults    97

## Parenthood and grandparenthood    109

## School and growing up    115

## Teens    127

## Celebrating friendship    137

| Key to symbols | |
| --- | --- |
| ✞ | Prayer |
| 🖋 | Liturgy |
| ((◎)) | Responsive prayer |
| ♫ | Song/Music |
| ✿ | Reflective prayer |
| ▥ | Reflection |
| ✖ | Poem |
| 🖎 | Story |
| 𝄇 | Reading |
| 🚲 | Practical |

## Breakdown of relationships    191

## Home    209

## Work and unemployment    221

| Key to symbols | |
|---|---|
| ✝ | Prayer |
| 🖋 | Liturgy |
| ((◉)) | Responsive prayer |
| ♫ | Song/Music |
| ☼ | Reflective prayer |
| 🏛 | Reflection |
| ✈ | Poem |
| 🖎 | Story |
| ᕬ | Reading |
| 🚲 | Practical |

Key to symbols

✝ Prayer
☙ Liturgy
((◦)) Responsive prayer
♫ Song/Music
☼ Reflective prayer
▦ Reflection
✗ Poem
▧ Story
ᏜᎧ Reading
🚲 Practical

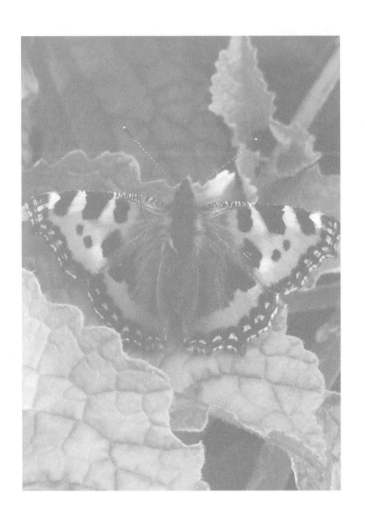

For Sarah
with love

## Introduction

*Moments of Our Nights and Days* is a resource book for anyone who is planning a baptism, naming ceremony, wedding or civil partnership. It also contains resources to mark many of the other significant moments of our nights and days.

It is likely that not everyone present at these moments will have a conventional religious faith: there are resources here that do not assume a faith commitment, as well as resources that reflect Christian belief.

Although a number of complete liturgies are included, most of the material consists of the stuff that liturgies are made of: responses, readings, rituals, actions, biblical reflections, poems, songs and prayers.

Whilst this book was being edited the celebration of partnerships has broadened in Britain and some of the pieces might today have been given less specific titles.

*Moments of Our Nights and Days* is a companion book to *Saying Goodbye*, a resource book for funerals which was published by Wild Goose Publications in 2013.

I am grateful to all the contributors to this book for their skill, sensitivity and imagination and for the rich and varied material that they have created; also for their patience: this book has been a long time coming.

Thanks are due to the Wild Goose Publications team: Sandra Kramer, Jane Darroch Riley, Alex O'Neill and Susie Hay. Particular thanks to Neil Paynter for his encouragement and legendary attention to detail.

*Keep us alert on our journeying, God:*
*full of wonder*
*strong in your strength*
*cherished in our weakness.*

*Summon us to live*
*in your loving justice*
*with friend and with stranger*
*and with those we find hard to love.*

*In bad times and good times*
*you are always with us,*
*Gifter of the moments*
*of our nights and days.*

Ruth Burgess, summer 2014

# Approaching birth

## Annunciation

Annunciation.
Stunned and awful silence.
The angel paused, expectant,
awaiting the reply.

Heaven held its breath.
And Mary …
Mary felt it slowly
take over every fibre of her being.

At first it seemed like fear
and she felt herself instinctively resist.
But as it seeped deeper
into her flesh and bones,
she knew herself
finally at home:
at one with joy.

Her Yes sparkled in her eyes, dancing its assent,
long before it reached her lips.
And Gabriel laughed aloud, winging homeward,
herald of such wondrous news.

Mary Hanrahan

## Pregnancy

Little one,
you have taken part of me
and yet belong only to yourself.
We are linked mysteriously, intimately,
yet we are separate beings.
I feel your strangeness in my body;
a differentness that is not me.
I feed you, enclose you and welcome you
until you become whole
and ready to make your journey.

Mary Hanrahan

# A question of a name

We need to think about a name.

Do we go for remembering a family member?
And, if we do, which family member do we choose?
Do we go Celtic, Gothic, ancient Egyptian?
Do we consult this year's Favourite Names List?
Do we go for a character we like in a film or book?
Do we say names out loud? Listen to how they sound?
Do we make up a name?
Or do we wait till the child is born
and then decide which name fits?

Do we look at a dictionary of names?
Do we look not only at names, but at their origins and meanings?
Or do we really want to know that the name we have chosen for our child
is probably derived from an ancient word for camel-keeper,
or that we are naming our child after a god of fire and destruction?
Probably not!

As our child grows
will he or she appreciate our choice?
Is the name we have chosen pronounceable,
easy to learn, to speak, to spell?
Is it familiar, or will it be a name that no one has ever heard of?
Does this name invite a nickname – and is the nickname nice?
Will this name work for a teenager, an adult, as well as for a child? ...

Child,
you are coming into the world soon.
We pray that we will give you a name
in which you,
and all who meet you,
can delight.

Ruth Burgess

# Birth and birth blessings

## Rounded walls

Inside, you built me.
You pushed back walls, made more room for your own growing.
You demanded foundations, tested them with your concentrating feet.
You stretched up, making rafters of my ribs,
pushing into the tenderness under my heart.

For you, I became a space, a home with rounded walls,
taut as a bowl, a full sail, holding us both
in our growing season.

There is a northern church with rounded walls,
a curved sunlit craft with no corners,
no places where one might hide.
But you, hidden in me, rounded me.
You gave me limits and lived within them.
You tumbled in me like a rock in the ocean,
curled into me like a fossil fish,
a growing bone.
Heavy in turmoil, heavy in rest.
And sometimes together we danced.

I wrapped my arms around my solid self and held on to you.

Days passed, weeks and our dance grew slower.
So did we.
We counted, climbed stairs, counted each one, slowly.
Then, the day came at bright noon when the rhythm grew insistent,
bringing us together suddenly turning.

And into that night, that long night, that started with insistent joy
we learned this new rhythm, calling rhythm,
working with arms wrapped around me, walls around to support me,
in a room set aside, a dwelling place, working place.
Beneath me a solid floor, and women's words whispered fathoms deep,
as you quaked inside me, I called out and together we grew;
uncertain, unstable, unsettled, rocked and raw.
Hands gripping, grabbing, fingers clenched as we tried hard to open,
me to you and you through me, opening into what dawn?

But dawn came, quietly, and you turned once more and
slipped through into warm hands, touch and new cloth.

And then the sounds of the world seeped through the curtains,
the open window,
slow rain stopping and the sound of birds on branches,
the sun not yet,
but we are.

I find you in my arms and outside these walls,
the world begins.
But no.
The world begins here.
In my arms, you look in my eyes, tying us two together.
The cord cut; there are cords newly there,
knitting us together as we need each other now,
weaving us to the world, those around, those outside.

I will need others now, more than before,
and you will welcome them, trust them, my love.
They too will love you.
This is how we make the world a home.

Katie Munnik


## Tom

Surprising as the snow
you exploded into the world
trailing fire and passion and pain,
yet smelling of stars, of the clean, crisp air
and earthy newness.

Welcome to this wide, white world:
to robins and red berries,
to elephants, giraffes and sunsets
and big aeroplanes.

May you be safe yet curious
as you watch the world change and grow,
every day, as you do,
forever wrapped in a shawl of amazement.

Mary Hanrahan

## For Kira

The sun was setting.

As a July day drew to a close
you were drawing near to taking your first breath.

Labour pains signalled the life
soon to transform our lives –
so long prayed for,
so much hoped for,
so long awaited.

Outside the hospital
the darkness of night deepened;
inside
worried glances,
staff filling the room,
concern that all was not well.

But then our fear
gave way to tears as you quietly entered the world:
tears of relief,
tears of an overwhelming happiness,
tears of the deepest love
that I have ever known.

In silence you rested in your mother's arms.

I left you both to sleep
and made my way home.

The sun was rising.

Simon Taylor

## A blessing on Henry, my first grandchild

May you give and receive love.
May you trust and be trusted.
May you dare and be daring.
May you believe and be believed.
And may you live in God's sunlight all your days.
Amen

Jean Williams


## A nontraditional blessing

May God bless you with *discontent* at easy answers, half-truths, superficial relationships, so that you will live from deep within your heart.

May God bless you with *anger* at injustice, oppression, abuse and exploitation of people, so that you will work for justice, equality and peace.

May God bless you with *tears* to shed for those who suffer from pain, rejection, starvation and war, so that you will reach out your hand to comfort them and to change their pain to joy.

May God bless you with the *foolishness* to think you can make a difference in this world, so that you will do the things which others tell you cannot be done.

Ruth Fox, OSB (Sacred Heart Monastery, Richardton, ND, USA)

## Open your heart

Open your heart, O God,
and pour out your gifts upon this baby.

Open your mouth, Lord Jesus,
that your words sing in *his/her* soul.

Open your hands, Holy Spirit,
and cradle *him/her* in your love,
that *he/she* might reach out
to receive every joy you have in store,
and be a blessing to all for evermore.

Thom M. Shuman


## Three days born

Outside
in the city streets
it was misty and cold.

But here, in the warm,
in a hospital cradle,
tiny thumbs and fingers
clutch at the air
and ruffle soft white cloth.

Three days born,
new life,
crying in the night.

God bless you,
little one,
little miracle of life.

Now,
and all the journey
of your nights
and days.

Ruth Burgess

## So, here you are, born

What are you like?
With your shiny face,
wee red legs
and wrinkled feet.

In this warm hospital, with its filtered air,
peaceful environment and calm nurses,
lying in the arms of your contented mum;
your dad, grannie and grandpa sitting round you
reaching out trying to pour health, love, safety,
into such a small vulnerable receptacle.

And when I held you,
trying to communicate my stuck feelings,
I fancied for a moment we met,
touching at a sigh
beyond my clumsy intellect.
And I wished for you
a future in which
no thoughtless human act will harm you,
so that I never fear for you,
so that I'm not crucified by my love,
so that your life will know days
of laughter and enchantment
and that a higher power will always
watch over you.

Actually, considering how small you are,
pound for pound you're more dangerous than Goliath,
reaching deep inside, touching parts
that have lay hidden for years.
Seven pounds two ounces of nothing
skipping adeptly over my stout defences,
flooding me with tears and love.
Listen! very few big folk can do that to me,
never mind a wee blade like you.
Did you think my heart did not thrill?

So welcome to the world, Natasha,
it's full of dirt and pain and fear,
but every now and then you'll meet an individual

who'll give you such a surge of loving respect
that (for a change) it makes you proud to be human.
Every now and then
you'll get what I got when I met you, Natasha:
a quiet rush of love and joy.

Stuart Barrie

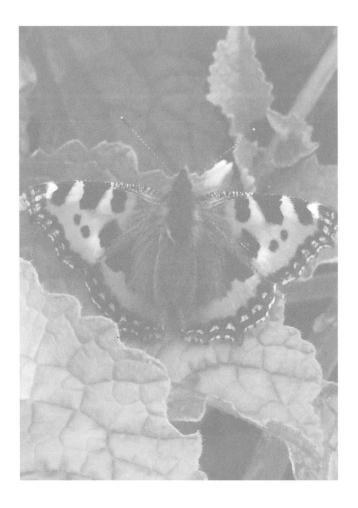

# Adoption

## Blessing at the placement of a child for adoption*

The blessing of God be on these parents
who brought this child into life
giving *him/her* love and talents.

The blessing of God be on these parents
who receive *him/her* into their lives
promising *him/her* love and nurture.

The blessing of God be on this child:
surrendered in love and pain,
received in love and joy.

The blessing of God be on us all,
the blessing of love unending.
The blessing of hope and life.

Pat Welburn

*Where appropriate, the names of the parents and child can be used.*

## Blessing for an adoptive family

God bless the family who adopted my son,
for giving him what I never could have done.
Bless his new mother and father,
his new brother and sister too.
I wish all God's blessings to follow you.

Linda Fraser

# Service of thanksgiving after adoption

*Before the service the children and parents gather signs and symbols of their love for each other and the life they share (e.g. flowers, a cooking pot, photos, a painting …)*

*A and B: the names of the adopted children*
*C and D: the names of the adoptive parents*

Opening responses:

When we are happy,
when we are full of fun and laughter,
GOD WELCOMES US

When we are searching,
when we are full of ideas and questions,
GOD WELCOMES US

When we are tired,
when we need to stop and rest and wonder,
GOD WELCOMES US

Alone, together,
with friends, with family
GOD WELCOMES US WITH LOVE.

Song

Prayer of approach and confession:

You welcome us here God, Star-maker, Dreamer.
You love us and we are grateful.
You warm us in the sunlight.
You delight us with snowflakes and steam engines and stones.
You call us by name and create us in your image.
You hold us strong in mystery and grace.

You call us here Jesus, Carpenter, Immanuel.
You have walked on earth.
You grew up in a family.
You know what life is like for us and we are grateful.
You challenge us and nourish us.
You make us smile with your stories.
You draw us deep into healing and justice.
You offer us friendship and joy.

You are among us here, Holy Spirit, Comforter, Disturber.
You are alive in us and we are grateful.
You nudge us and question us.
You call us your children.
You quicken us in the wildness of your dancing.
You wrap us round securely in the shawl of your love.

In this place and this moment we are here, God,
caught up in the song and stories,
caught up with the stars and the angels and saints,
rejoicing in the warmth of your welcome,
grateful that you are here with us.

You know us, God,
all our lives you have known us:
you know our fears and our questions,
you know the dark and light in us,
you know our hunger and our love.

Here in the silence of your loving
and in the company of your people
we bring you the things that trouble us,
that hurt and harm us and others,
that make us less than the people you want us to be …

God have mercy on us.
Christ have mercy on us.

Listen to the words of Jesus,
words that we can trust:

*'Don't be afraid.*
*I love you.*
*I forgive you.*
*You are my friends.*
*Come and follow me.'*

Thanks be to God.
AMEN

**Song/psalm**

**Readings:** Ephesians 3:14–21, and a story of belonging (e.g. *Ivor the Engine: The First Story*)*

A creed

Prayers of thanksgiving:

We thank God for bringing A and B into this family.

God our Maker,
we thank you for the wonder and joy of creation.
We thank you for the lives of A and B,
made in your image
blessed with your love.

*The adoptive parents say together:*

God our Father,
thank you for these children.
Help us to be good parents.
Make us patient and understanding.
May our children be sure of our love.
May we grow together as a family,
through Jesus Christ our Lord.
Amen

Reading: Mark 10:13–16

*A and B are given a book of Bible stories:*

We give you these books which tell the story of God's love and goodness.
We pray that your family life may be rooted in justice and love.

The Lord's Prayer

The placing of signs and symbols:

We invite A, B, C and D to place on the central table signs and symbols of their love for each other and the life they share.

*(Symbols are placed.)*

And we invite them to light a candle to give thanks for the light of God in their lives.

*(A candle is lit.)*

Prayers:

God, look on this family.
Be amongst them.
May they grow together in hope and love.

*A prayer to be said by the wider members of A and B's new family:*

We receive these children into our family with joy.
Through God's love we will care for them,
we will be there for them,
we will guide them in God's way.
Amen

*A prayer to be said by all:*

GOD BLESS THIS FAMILY AND ITS NEWEST MEMBERS.
HELP US TO SUPPORT THEM IN PRAYER AND ACTION.
HELP THEM TO LIVE TOGETHER IN LOVE AND JUSTICE
AND TO SHARE THEIR LOVE WITH THOSE IN NEED.
AMEN

Song

Prayers of intercession:

Let us pray for our needs and the needs of God's world …

We pray for our own families, for parents, children, grandparents,
sisters, brothers, grandchildren, aunts and uncles and cousins …
God in your mercy …
HEAR OUR PRAYER.

We pray for A and B's natural family, that God may bless them
and give them love and peace …
God in your mercy …
HEAR OUR PRAYER.

We pray for families where there is sickness or need or hunger …
God in your mercy …
HEAR OUR PRAYER.

We pray for families and close relationships where there is breakdown and pain …
God in your mercy …
HEAR OUR PRAYER.

We pray for families where life is good and love is celebrated and shared …
God in your mercy …
HEAR OUR PRAYER.

We pray for parents who have lost a child and couples unable to have children …
God in your mercy …
HEAR OUR PRAYER.

We pray for friends who know what we care about and who share our smiles and tears …
God in your mercy …
HEAR OUR PRAYER.

We pray for those who live in community, and those who live alone …
God in your mercy …
HEAR OUR PRAYER.

We pray for ourselves, that we may live in God's peace and justice.
May we enjoy the love of friends and family.
May we get to know strangers.
May we delight in the friendship and glory of God.
AMEN

Closing responses:

*(To be said alternately by 2 parts/sides of the congregation)*

*A:* God bless us and our families:
*B:* GIVE US COURAGE AND KEEP US LOVING.

*A:* God help us to live in truth:
*B:* TO STAND BY THOSE WHO NEED OUR HELP.

*A:* God give us friends who love us:
*B:* PEOPLE AND PLACES THAT HELP US GROW.

*A:* God send us on our way rejoicing.
*B:* MAY WE ALWAYS WALK IN THE LIGHT OF YOUR LOVE.

Blessing

A lively song to leave

Ruth Burgess, with thanks to Andrew, Amanda, David and Billy, who are into steam engines and stones

* Ivor the Engine: The First Story, *by Oliver Postgate, Severnside Wholesalers Limited, 2006*

# Baptism and naming ceremonies for young children

# The blessing of a child (without baptism)

**Opening responses:**

In the beginning, God made the world,
light and dark, shape and void, height and depth,
to tell of love.
AND GOD SAYS IT IS GOOD.

In land and sea, in plant and seed,
in growth and decay,
God's love is shown.
AND GOD SAYS IT IS GOOD.

In creatures great and small,
in movement and stillness, in birth and death,
God's love is shown.
AND GOD SAYS IT IS GOOD.

In woman and man,
in joy and sorrow, in laughter and tears,
God's love is shown.
AND GOD SAYS IT IS GOOD.

In the gift of new life, in signs of hope,
in the children we are given,
God's love is shown.
AND GOD SAYS IT IS GOOD.

So let us celebrate and give thanks
for the gift of this child.
WITH GOD WE SAY, 'IT IS GOOD.'

Jesus said: 'Let the children come to me;
do not try to stop them,
for the kingdom of heaven belongs to such as these.'

**Song**

**Prayer:**

God our Maker,
we praise you for your creation,

and especially for life new and renewed.
We rejoice and thank you for the life of *(name)*
given in love to
*(name)* and *(name)* as their child.
We pray that *(name)* and *(name)* will,
in their loving, guiding and nurturing of their child,
be strengthened and aided by the power and presence of your love
in Jesus Christ.
Amen

*Leader:*

*(Name)* and *(name)*, will you, with God's help, strive to share your love, faith, wisdom and understanding with *(name)* and make for *her/him* a home where *she/he* may learn to live in love, peace and justice?

*Parents/carers:*

We will.

*Leader:*

Will you who form the community of love in which *(name)* will grow, with God's help, keep this child and *her/his parents/carers* in your hearts and prayers, and give an example of faith, hope and love to them all?

*All:*

We will.

*The parents/carers are invited to bless the child:*

May God's joy be in your heart
and God's love surround your living,
each day and each night
and wherever you roam.

May you know God's presence:
in growing and learning,
in joy and sorrow,
in friendship and solitude,
in beginnings and endings
And may God bless you and keep you,
all the days of your life.

*Parents/carers kiss the child. A lit candle is placed near child:*

THE BRIGHT LIGHT OF GOD'S GUARDING BE WITH YOU.
THE BRIGHT LIGHT OF CHRIST'S LOVE BE WITH YOU.
THE BRIGHT LIGHT OF THE SPIRIT'S PRESENCE SURROUND AND ENFOLD YOU.
ALL THE DAYS AND NIGHTS OF YOUR LIFE. AMEN

**Song**

**Closing responses:**

Making us, shaping us,
BLESSING US, TRUSTING US,

Leading us, disturbing us,
EMPOWERING US, LOVING US,

God of our childhood,
GOD OF OUR GROWING,

Stay with us on our journey
AND BRING US SAFELY HOME.

Joanna Anderson

# Celebration of baptism

*Where one parent, B, is a Christian and the other, C, is not.*

**Song:** 'Ubi caritas et amor, Deus ibi est' ('Where charity and love are, God is there')

*Leader (priest):*

What name have you chosen for your baby?

*B and C:*

*(Her/his)* name is _____.

*Leader:*

What do you want for this child?

*B and C:*

We want *her/him* to grow up seeking after truth and to do what is right.

We want *(name)* to be part of a loving family of relations and friends who will help *her/him* to do that.

*Leader:*

Why have you brought this child to be baptised?

*B and godparents:*

We want *(name)* to be a member of the Christian family, living and growing in the knowledge of God.

*The priest traces a cross on the baby's forehead with the water, and invites others to do the same.*

A blessing for a baby born in summer:

*(For alternative seasonal blessings see pp79-81)*

Welcome *(name)*.
You arrived with the summer roses,
petals unfolding, fragile and fragrant,
shaken by rainstorms,
warmed by the strengthening sun.

Welcome *(name)*:
May your life unfold in warmth and beauty.
May angels protect you and saints tell you stories.
May you be caressed and cherished.
May you be cradled in love.

Welcome *(name)*:
May you bring joy to all who meet you.
May you grow each day in grace and wonder.
May you be blessed with the wildness and wisdom of God.

Readings: John 16:21–22; Revelation 12:1–17

Prayers:

*Folk are invited to share prayers and wishes for the baby and for the world she/he will grow up in. After each prayer they may come forward and light a candle.*

Anointing before baptism:

*Leader:*

Jesus came among us to show us how to live – he came that we might have life and have it in abundance. We pray that, through his grace, *(baby's name)* may share fully in that life.

*The baby is anointed with oil.*

*Leader:*

*(Name)*, we anoint you with the oil of salvation. May God strengthen you with power and love.

Statements of belief:

*B and C:*

We believe in the dignity and value of all human beings.

We reject all the ways by which some human beings seek to separate and dehumanise others. We believe all humans are created equal and have a right to justice: enough food and water, a home to live in and the dignity of work.

We hope that *(name of child)*, through *her/his* decisions and life, will help to build an equitable world.

*B and godparents:*

We believe in a creating God who, out of love, brought the universe into being and who delights in the beauty of that creation.

We are made in the image of God and so share in God's capacity to love and be creative. *(name of child)* is a celebration of that love and creativity. As *she/he* grows we will share with *her/him* the beauty and wonder of the universe, hoping that *she/he* recognises the beauty and wonder of the Creator reflected in it.

We believe in a redeeming God who, in Jesus, came among us and shared our humanity. A God who chose to be with those on the margins of society – the poor, the outcasts.

We believe in Jesus, who first told of his messiahship to a woman at a well, and who first showed his risen self to a woman. Through his resurrection we are all offered hope and the possibility of transformation. Like the woman of Samaria and Mary of Magdala, we are called to share that hope with others. Today we share that hope with *(baby's name)*. We will support and encourage *her/him* as *she/he* grows older so that hope may be a reality in *her/his* life.

We believe in a sustaining God who is with us still, breathing life into creation. We believe that this sustaining Spirit renews us and challenges us to reach out to all people and to work to build a world of justice, healing and wholeness.

We believe that God is present in the church, the institutional church and in us, the community of believers, sustaining us and leading us forward. In having *(name)* baptised, we are welcoming *her/him* into this community. We will try to help *her/him* become a full member of it.

**Baptism:**

*B and the godparents join the priest in pouring water on the baby's head, while all present say:*

(NAME), WE BAPTISE YOU IN THE NAME OF GOD OUR FATHER,
WHO CREATED THE UNIVERSE.
IN THE NAME OF JESUS HIS SON,
WHO CAME AMONG US AS OUR REDEEMER.
AND IN THE NAME OF THE HOLY SPIRIT,
WHO IS WITH US NOW, SUSTAINING OUR FAITH.

**Anointing with chrism (consecrated oil):**

*The priest anoints the baby on the head with chrism while saying:*

*(Name)*, as a member of the Christian community, you are called to become like Christ. The word Christ means 'the anointed one'. I now anoint you with chrism as a sign of you being truly Christed, or christened.

Robing:

*The priest puts a white robe on the baby, saying:*

*(Name)*, you have become a new creation, clothed in Christ. This white garment is the outward sign of your Christian dignity. With your family and friends to help you, may you grow in goodness and truth. Amen

Sign of peace

Lighting of a candle:

*B lights a candle and gives it to the baby, saying:*

Receive the light of Christ.

Blessing:

May God, who laboured in love to create all life,
continue creating within us new hope,
new joy, new visions;
and may we go from here to bring
new life to the world.
Amen

*(by Dorothy Brooker and others)*

Song: 'We shall go out with hope of resurrection', by June Boyce-Tillman (Stainer and Bell)

Brid Fitzpatrick, Campbell Macaulay and Ruth Burgess, with thanks to Lorna and Eben for whom the liturgy was written

# Naming ceremonies

*Adapt these resources to your circumstances.*

### A blessing and candlelit offering from the parents:

Beloved *(name)*, so we name you. In love you were born and in love you shall grow. Let the light of these candles be a symbol of the light of our undying love for you and of our promise to cherish you, all the days of our lives.

### A blessing and candlelit offering from an older sibling:

My dear *(sister/brother)*, I am looking forward to growing up with you. May I be the best *(brother/sister)* I can be for you, and here is my gift of love to you *(lights candle)*.

### A blessing and candlelit offering from the grandparents:

We pledge to love and keep you and to share our wisdom and strength in the service of you and your parents. Let the light of these candles be a symbol of the light of our love in your life.

### A blessing and candlelit offering from the godparents:

*(Name)*, we promise to love and support you and your parents as you grow, to be available to you in time of need, and to be your faithful guides and guardians as you find your chosen path. This candle is a demonstration of our lifelong commitment to you.

### A blessing from a family elder (based on an African tradition):

*The elder takes a little lemon juice, places it on the lips of the child, and says the following:*

Life in this world is sometimes bitter. We pray that such times will be few for you and that, when they do arise, they only serve to strengthen your commitment to loving.

*A little honey is placed on the lips of the child:*

May your life be rich in happiness and plentiful sweet blessings.

*A little wine is placed on the lips of the child:*

We pray that the joy and love you have awakened in us, simply by your presence, will flow back to you throughout your life – multiplied beyond measure.

*The wine is passed around:*

We drink in celebration of the joy of life and the commitment to support and encourage this child to make the best of whatever life will bring.

**An interfaith blessing:**

Many traditions speak of the four sacred elements: earth, air, fire and water ...

*(Name)*, we bring you the gift of earth *(sand, pebbles, stones, a flower in a pot ...)*.

May you live long in health and vitality and in the awareness and joy of your body.

We bring you the gift of air *(a kite, balloon...)*.

May your life be filled with the expression of the highest and most noble ideals of mind and spirit.

We bring you the gift of fire *(a candle, lamp ...)*.

May you fully express your creativity, bringing joy and fulfilment to yourself and everyone you meet.

We bring you the gift of water *(a glass of water, water poured from one container to another, water sprinkled on the child and gathering...)*.

May you discover and learn to express the depth of your emotions as you connect ever-more profoundly with yourself and others down the years.

And there is a fifth element: Love. It is ever-present and it binds the whole universe together. It is the same element that binds your parents to you. You are the child of your parents and of the universe and of that greatest Love. You are bound to everyone in the world by this gentlest and strongest of bonds. May awareness of your true nature be present in and around you all the days of your life.

We bring you the gift of Love *(a kiss, hug ...)*.

**Creating a time capsule:**

*Relatives and friends are asked to bring a letter or small gift for the child to be placed in a time capsule (a jewellery box, etc).*

May these gifts be blessed.
May they be a source of wonder and joy
when *(name)* reaches 18 years of age.
I call upon everyone present to make a vow in support of *(name)*:
Do you promise to help and support *(name)* and *her/his* parents in love and wisdom

so that *(name)* is raised well and lovingly?

*All:* We do.

*Candles are lit …*

*The box is sealed up (with the candles) and buried/stored until the child's 18th birthday, when it is opened by the person and the candles are re-lit …*

Stephen Wright

# Naming grandchildren

*This service is intended for those whose grandchildren have not been, and are unlikely to be, baptised.*

*Sit together in a circle, with a candle, bowl of water and cross in the centre. A supply of tea-lights is needed for the prayers.*

Praise to God who made us,
PRAISE TO GOD WHO IS BESIDE US,
Praise to God who is within us.

**Song of praise**

**Opening prayer:**

Living God,
we thank you for the gift of grandchildren.
For their promise of new life,
for the potential we see in them,
for the joy they give us.
WE THANK YOU GOD. AMEN

**Bible reading:** e.g. Mark 10:13–16

This is the word of the Lord.
THANKS BE TO GOD.

**Poems**

**Sharing:**

*Grandparents share something about their grandchild – a story, memory – and then place a picture of them around the candle in the centre; as they do, they 'name' the child.*

**Prayers:**

Holy Spirit,
bless these little ones:
bless their growing,
bless their sleeping.
WE WELCOME YOU *(NAME OF CHILD)*
AND WE WELCOME THE HOLY SPIRIT WITHIN YOU.

Jesus Christ,
bless these little ones:
bless their knowing,
bless their journey.
WE WELCOME YOU *(NAME OF CHILD)*
AND WE WELCOME THE SON OF GOD BESIDE YOU.

Loving Creator,
bless these little ones:
bless their playing,
bless their parents.
AWAKEN YOUR LOVE WITHIN THEM.

Holy God,
we name these children before you:
bless them, shield them, hold them.
MAY THEY HEAR YOUR VOICE WITHIN THEM. AMEN

*Each grandparent then lights a tea-light from the central candle and makes a specific prayer for their grandchild, out loud or silently.*

**Prayers:**

Living God,
we pray for the parents of these children *(parents' names can be said).*
Bless them in mothering and fathering:
help them direct these new lives
with your love and wisdom.
Strengthen them when they are weary,
protect them from all that harms

and open their hearts to your love.
HEAR OUR PRAYER, THAT THEY MAY COME TO KNOW YOU. AMEN

Bless us, Living God:
teach us when to speak, and when to be silent;
when to offer help, and when to leave things alone.
Grant us the wisdom to accept different practices –
and thank you for the fun of playing and laughing
with our grandchildren.
BLESS US, LIVING GOD. AMEN

**Sung blessing:** ('The peace of the earth be with you', from *There Is One Among Us*, John L. Bell, Wild Goose Publications)

*All share the peace.*

Chris Polhill


# Blessing of a child at a family gathering

*A: name of the child*

*B and C: names of the parents*

*Leader:*

We come to ask God's blessing on A, and on B and C as they seek God's blessing on A, all the days and moments of *(his/her)* life, and as they seek God's continuing grace as they adjust to the joys and challenges of being parents in the days ahead.

B and C, in asking for God's blessing on A, do you promise at all times to love, cherish and support *(him/her)* and, so far as you are able, to teach *(him/her)* to pursue what is good, true, lovely and just: to care for others and to lead a life of integrity?

*B and C:*

We do.

*Leader:*

A, may God's richest blessing be upon you. May God's love surround you, God's grace sustain you and God's hope inspire you all the days of your life.

God bless you and keep you. May God's face shine upon you; may God be gracious to you, lift up his countenance upon you and give you peace, this day and always. Amen

Loving God, as we pray for A, we pray also for your blessing on B and C, as they face the inevitable ups and downs of the days ahead.

May they know that your everlasting arms are always there, ready to love, support and guide them in the way of compassion and joy.

Bless also the wider family gathered here, and B and C's wider circle of friends, that we may at all times be ready to support B and C, and that we too, in your grace, may be guided and strengthened to lead lives that are for the good of all.

We ask this in Jesus' name. Amen

Norman Shanks

## Baptism in church

*A: name of the child*

*B and C: names of the parents*

**Welcome**

*Leader:*

From the start of Christian community centuries ago, people have been received into the church through baptism. Baptism is a sign that God loves each one of us individually. It shows and tells us that God's love encompasses and embraces us all and that God's grace works in and through our lives. The water we use in baptism is thus a seal of God's grace and reminds us of Jesus Christ, who was himself baptised, buried and raised that we might know life in all its fullness. The water is sprinkled, poured out – like God's Spirit – on us and for us all so we are reminded and assured that we are all God's children, that our future lies with God, and that the church, the family of God, is where we will be helped and equipped to serve God in the world.

*The parents, godparents, family and friends come forward with the child.*

*Leader:*

B and C, in bringing A for baptism, do you confess your faith in God, the loving Creator, in Jesus Christ, in and through whom we are promised life, and in the Holy Spirit, our helper and guide?

*B and C:*

We do.

*Leader:*

Loving God, as you have called us to share in your grace and love in the fellowship of faith, so we receive this little *(girl/boy)* to be baptised in your name. By the power of your Holy Spirit, present with us now, may A receive the fullness of your grace and remain faithful to you all of *(her/his)* days, through Jesus Christ our Lord. Amen.

A, I baptise you in the name of the Father, and of the Son, and of the Holy Spirit. May the peace of God fill your heart, the hope of God shape your thinking, and the love of God direct your life. Amen

## Question for the parents:

*Leader:*

B and C, do you promise, with God's help, to continue to provide a loving home for A and to bring *(her/him)* up in the faith of the Gospel and, so far as you are able, in the fellowship of the church?

*B and C:*

We do.

## Question for congregation:

*Leader:*

Do you, as the congregation of this church, and as the wider family and friends of B and C, promise to do all you can to care for A and to encourage and support *(her/his)* parents in keeping the promises they have made, so that A may grow in grace and in the knowledge and love of God? Please show your assent by standing …

**Song:** 'The Lord bless you and keep you' (CH4 796)

*Leader:*

According to Christ's commandment, A is now received into the family and household of God. May God help us all to keep our promises.

**Prayer:**

Living God, we thank you that A is now part of the life of the church. Grant that *(she/he)* may grow in grace, come to know that *(she/he)* is kept always in your love, and be strengthened in faith.

We ask your special blessing on *(her/his)* family: that B and C may know that they are surrounded with love that is secure and gentle and may be given the grace and wisdom to teach A your truth and lead *(her/him)* in the way of your loving self-giving.

Touch us all with the promise of this sacrament – with a spirit of joy and hope that enables us to face the future with courage and cheerfulness, trusting always in your loving purpose, through Jesus Christ our Lord. Amen

Norman Shanks

# A service for the anointing of a child

*This ceremony is for parents who are looking for something that is more than an act of thanksgiving and that feels more relevant to them than the somewhat archaically worded and formal Sacrament of Baptism.*

*I recognise that this liturgy will not 'count' as baptism, and that parents who want the certified version do have to accept the requirements of the Churches in that respect.*

*In the service, I have retained anointing with oil (a practice that is used in some baptism services) but have avoided the use of water in order to clarify that this is not baptism.*

*For ease of reading I have used feminine pronouns and written for one child: adapt as necessary.*

*A and B: names of the parents*

*C: name of the child*

Introduction:

*Leader:*

Welcome to this ceremony of anointing.

The service follows a pattern similar to that of Christian baptism. It differs from the Sacrament of Baptism in that it allows the parents to choose what promises they make to their child.

The service is in three parts: we begin with some questions about the nature of this ceremony and commitments to the child; we then have two short Bible readings about the origins of Christian baptism and prayers for the child; and we conclude with the ceremony of anointing and the giving of a candle.

The questions and commitments:

*Leader:*

We now come to questions that will give A and B the opportunity to tell us a bit about why we are here today.

A and B, you have brought C here to give thanks for her birth. What led you to bring her?

*A and B:*

We are grateful for the gift of C:
for the new life she brings,
for the hope she represents,
for the joy of being parents.

*Leader:*

What concerns do you have as parents?

*A and B:*

We are concerned that we will not always know what is best for C,
that we may not always choose what is best for her,
that there may be difficulties that we have not foreseen.

*Leader:*

What hopes do you have as parents?

*A and B:*

We hope that we will be honest about our mistakes.

That we will be there when our child needs us,
that we will ask for help when we need it,
that our child will know that we love her.

*Leader (to the godparents):*

You have agreed to be godparents to C.
What do you understand by that commitment?

*Godparents:*

We will support A and B in their parenting.
We will pray for the family regularly.

We will be adult friends to support C on life's journey.
C will always be special to us.

*Leader (to parents):*

Why have you chosen to have this ceremony in a Christian place of worship?

*A and B:*

We believe and trust that God, the source of all life,
came in human form as Jesus of Nazareth,
taught us how to live,
died for us,
and rose again.
We want to ask for God's help as we bring up our child.

*Leader:*

How do you believe God will offer you that help?

*A and B:*

We believe that God's Holy Spirit will act through us if we place our trust in God and open our hearts to understand God's will for us.

*Leader:*

How will you keep your heart open to God?

*A and B:*

We will acknowledge that we make mistakes.

We will ask God to forgive us, and to help us forgive ourselves.
We will seek help and advice from others whom we trust.

*Leader:*

Family, godparents, friends and church members, are you willing to offer that help?

*ALL:*

WITH GOD'S HELP, WE ARE.

**Bible readings and prayers for the child:**

Reading 1: An account of Jesus' baptism (e.g. Matthew 3:13–17)

Reading 2: An account of baptism in the early church (e.g. Acts 8:12–17 or Acts 16:11–15)

*Leader:*

Creator God, we give thanks for the gift of life: for your gift of life to each of us here today and especially for the gift of C. May we be worthy of this gift, and cherish life in all its amazing forms.

Grant to A and B the love, wisdom and insight they need to offer C the fullness of life they seek for her. Grant to us the sense to recognise when our help is needed, and when it is not.

*ALL:*

AMEN

*The parents may wish to read a prayer or poem they have written or chosen.*

**Ceremony of anointing and the giving of a candle:**

*Leader:*

This oil was blessed at … *(ceremony if relevant)* …

*Or:*

*Leader:*

Living God, make this oil special. We use it to affirm the promises we have made and to bless C.

*The leader makes the sign of the cross on the throat/hand of the child with the oil.*

C, we welcome you into God's family, we affirm the name you have been given, and we pray that your life will be blessed and be a blessing to others. In the name of God, Creator, Carer and Friend.

Blessing:

MAY GOD'S JOY BE IN YOUR HEART.
MAY GOD'S LOVE SURROUND YOUR LIVING,
EACH DAY AND EACH NIGHT,
WHEREVER YOU ARE.

MAY YOU RECOGNISE GOD'S PRESENCE
IN GROWING AND LEARNING,
IN JOY AND SORROW,
IN FRIENDSHIP AND LONELINESS,
IN BEGINNINGS AND ENDINGS.

MAY GOD KEEP YOU AND BLESS YOU
ALL THE DAYS OF YOUR LIFE.

*Leader (to the parents):*

As you go out from here, I give you this light *(lighted candle),* as a symbol of God's wisdom to light your journey, and as a prayer that C will be a light to you and to everyone she meets.

John Polhill

# An order of service for the baptism/naming/dedication of a child

Why have we come here today?
To link with tradition?
To tap into something spiritual?
To ask a blessing on this child?
To bring *her/him* into a safe place?

Whether or not we can link with church traditions,
whether or not we are sure if we believe in God,
whether or not this place has any significance for us:
we come here and now for the sake of this child.

This child is our special responsibility.
We love *her/him*.
We want to do all we can to keep *her/him* safe and protected.
So we bring *her/him* into this place for the tradition of *baptism/naming/dedication*,
believing that, in some way, this act will give a blessing on this child's life.

Whether or not we believe in God, God believes in us.
This child is special to you and to God.
Each of us is a unique and valued child of God.

So, as we offer this child for God's blessing, we remember that God welcomes and blesses all children, of whatever age or belief.

God understands children.

Jesus was born into a family home and grew up in the care of human parents.

Jesus welcomed children and said that their loving, trusting attitude was exactly what was needed for those who wish to follow his way in trying to change the world.

So we bring this child for God's blessing and we make promises for *her/his* future.

To all of you who love this child – parents, relatives, friends – we ask: Do you promise to love this child and to do your best to provide a safe and loving space for *her/him*?

WE PROMISE TO DO THAT, AS FAR AS WE ARE ABLE.

Do you promise to help this child to develop in every way: in body, mind and spirit?

WE PROMISE TO DO THAT, AS FAR AS WE ARE ABLE.

Will you remember this day as a special one? Will you explain its meaning to *her/him* and offer *her/him* the opportunity to talk about and explore what happened to *her/him* today when *she/he* is older?

WE PROMISE TO DO THAT, AS FAR AS WE ARE ABLE.

Will all those who are here to support the family of this child promise to offer help, encouragement and care, as *she/he* grows and develops.

WE PROMISE TO DO THAT, AS FAR AS WE ARE ABLE.

Will all those here who believe in God promise to offer a ready welcome and an opportunity for discovery to this child, and to all who wish to explore issues of faith?

WE PROMISE TO DO THAT, AS FAR AS WE ARE ABLE AND WITH THE HELP OF GOD.

Now we bring this child for *baptism/naming/dedication* and to ask God's blessing on *her/his* life.

*To the parent(s)/guardians:* What name have you given this child?

*Parent(s) or guardians give name.*

*Either:*

We baptise/name you *(name)* and ask for God's blessing on your life.

*or:*

We dedicate *(name)*, thanking God for *her/his* life and asking for blessing upon it.

God blesses you and holds you.
May you know God's love as a reality in your life.
AMEN

A song of celebration

Let us celebrate this life and give thanks for *(name)*.

*(Singing, applause, handshakes, a parade around the church, or whatever other action seems appropriate at this point)*

Marjorie Dobson

# A welcoming blessing for children already baptised

*Adapt as necessary*

*A and B: names of the parents*

*C and D: names of the children*

This is a moment chosen by A and B in response to the gift of their children.
In this moment they celebrate the coming of C and D into their lives.
They come here to thank God for the wonder of their birth
and for the joy that is contained in their lives.
They are here to ask us in the church to share their joy
and on their behalf to ask God's blessing on C and D in their life's journey.

Their baptisms have already taken place in the Roman Catholic Church.
C was baptised two years ago in Kelvindale, Glasgow.
And just last month D was baptised in the Church of the Holy Family here in Dunblane.
But it is their parents' wish that they may belong in both churches,
and so they come to the congregation in which B grew up
so that their place here may also be affirmed and acknowledged,
that this too might be their home.
This we gladly do, for Jesus said it was his express wish
that children should always be welcomed and blessed.

The story says:

*They were bringing children to Jesus that he might touch them, but the disciples rebuked them. When Jesus saw it, he was indignant and said: 'Let the children come to me; do not try to stop them; for the kingdom of God belongs to such as these.' And he took them up in his arms, laid his hands upon them and blessed them. (Mark 10:13–16)*

Today we ask that same blessing on C and D.

The promise:

Will the parents please stand.

In response to the miracle of life,
and aware that all of life is a gift,
do you seek God's blessing on the life of C
who has been given to you,
and do you promise to be faithful and loving parents
for as long as you have life?

*A and B:* We do.

The blessing:

C, in the name of Jesus Christ, I lay my hand upon you
and commend you to the care and love of God
through all your days.

May God's love enfold you. May he hold you forever in the palm of his hand.
May God's love embrace you. May you grow in grace and peace.

*(Repeat promise and blessing for child D)*

The congregation sings 'The Lord bless you and keep you'.

The welcome:

*(with the family facing the congregation)*

Welcome, C and D.
The whole world welcomes you,
you belong to the whole world.
You've been cradled in the warmth of your family's love,
you've been baptised into the wider family of God's love,
and now you're welcomed here in the care and friendship of this church.
So snuggle in, C and D.
You are safe.

Welcome, C.
Your mum and dad say you were an easy-going relaxed baby,
and now a good-humoured boy is emerging.
May your life now unfold in warmth and beauty.
May your growth be plentiful.
May the angels protect you and saints tell you stories.
May you be caressed and cherished and cradled in love.

Welcome, D.
Your mum and dad say you're very vocal in making your wants known,
that there's a cheerful and strong personality in you.
May you bring joy to all who meet you.
May you grow each day in grace and in wonder.
May you be blessed with the wildness and wisdom of God.

Prayer:

Hear us, God, as we pray for this family.
May all that is loving in the universe surround them.
May all that is strong and true and free walk with them.
May life fill them with joy.

Bless A and B as parents.
Go with them on their walk into the unknown future.
May they prepare their children to take their place as citizens of the world,
and prepare themselves one day to let them go.

With them, may we build a world that is safe and just
for all our children.
So may we all be blessed as we journey on our way,
and explore with daily-increasing wonder the paths of life.

May Jesus walk beside us on the way.
May the Spirit dance in the life that awaits us:
through Jesus Christ our Lord.
Amen

Colin McIntosh

Sentences and blessings for baptisms,
naming ceremonies and dedications

Jesus was baptised in the River Jordan by John.
And a voice from heaven said,
'You are my child. I love you. In you I take delight.'

Mark 1:9,11

I will sprinkle clean water on you.
I will give you a loving heart
and put my spirit in you.

Ezekiel 36:25a,26a

Jesus called the children to him,
took each one of them in his arms
and blessed them.

Mark 10:14,16

God is my shepherd.
He leads me along the right paths.
He leads me to deep still waters.

Psalm 23:1,2,3

A palmful of water of the God of life.
A palmful of water of the Christ of love.
A palmful of water of the Spirit of peace.

Carmina Gadelica (adapted)

A drop of water,
in the name of God the Maker,
for wisdom and wonder.

A drop of water,
in the name of Jesus,
for courage and justice.

A drop of water,
in the name of the Holy Spirit,
for curiosity and love.

Carmina Gadelica (adapted)

You created every part of me:
you put me together in my mother's womb.
When I was growing there in secret,
you knew that I was there –
you saw me before I was born.

Psalm 139:13,15b

You show your care for the land by sending rain;
you make it rich and fertile.
You fill the streams with water;
you provide the earth with crops.
This is how you do it:
you send abundant rain on the ploughed fields
and soak them with water;
you soften the soil with showers
and cause the young plants to grow.
What a rich harvest your goodness provides!

Psalm 65:9–11

Quiet Brigit
gentle Mary
warrior Michael
be aiding you.

Holy Apostles
courageous martyrs
glorious angels
be cherishing you.

God of the elements
Christ of the journey
Spirit of tenderness
be guarding you.

The Three all-knowing
be blessing you.

Carmina Gadelica (adapted)

As they travelled down the road
they came to a place where there was water.
And the Ethiopian said to Philip,
'Here is water.
What is there to keep me from being baptised?'

Acts 8:36

You make springs flow in the valleys
and rivers run between the hills.
You send rain from the sky
and the earth is filled with your blessings.

Psalm 104:10,13

A splash to keep you
a splash to aid you
a splash to circle you,
beloved one.

In the name of the Father
in the name of Jesus
in the name of the Spirit,
beloved one.

Be blessed with water
be blessed with wonder
be blessed all your journey,
beloved one.

Carmina Gadelica (adapted)

When, in the beginning, the God created human beings,
he left them free to do as they wished.
If you want to, you can keep the God's commands.
You can decide whether you will be loyal to him or not.
He has placed fire and water before you:
reach out and take whichever you want.
You have a choice between life and death;
you will get whichever you choose.

Sirach 15:14–17

May the King of Glory succour you.
May the Son of Mary safeguard you.
May the Holy Spirit satisfy you
with the living water of glory and grace.

Carmina Gadelica (adapted)

God spreads snow like a blanket
sends hail like gravel
and scatters frost like dust.

Then God gives a command
and the ice melts
and the water flows.

God tells out the number of the stars
and calls each one by name.

It is good to sing God's glory and praise.

Psalm 147:1,4,16–18

In the name of the Father, Son and Spirit,
Three all-kindly, Three all-holy,
may you be cherished, may you be aided,
may your feet be kept from stumbling.

Carmina Gadelica (adapted)

Sprinkle upon her your grace
that she may be filled with strength and wonder.
Put on her the water of meaning
that she may be filled with sense and reason.
And grant her angel wisdom
that she may stand in your presence
and rejoice.

Carmina Gadelica (adapted)

Jesus gives us freely of the water of life.

Revelation 22:17

Be each saint in heaven
each angel in heaven
stretching their arms for you
smoothing the way for you
east or west
wherever you go.

Carmina Gadelica (adapted)

May God give blessing
to the child that is here.

May Jesus give blessing
to the child that is here.

May Spirit give blessing
to the child that is here.

Plenty of food
much of mirth
plenty of kindness
much of life.

May the Three give blessing
to the child that is here.

Carmina Gadelica (adapted)

Jesus said, 'Go and make disciples and baptise them in the name of the Father,
and the Son, and the Holy Spirit.'

Matthew 28:19

Grow well child.
Enjoy the world.
Learn about your brothers and sisters everywhere.
Respect the universe.
Learn to share.
And be blessed by those who love you now
and will love you
in the coming years and days.

Ruth Burgess

Bits and pieces for baptisms, dedications, blessings and naming ceremonies

# Baptism is all about community (from a sermon)

Baptism is not a private family celebration. Baptism is all about community. Baptism makes us part of a community that is far bigger than we might ever imagine – a boundless community where everyone belongs – because baptism is about the kind of world we want our children and grandchildren to grow up in, and it's about what we're going to do to help bring that world into being and give the world back its hope.

In a world that values money more than anything else, we are meant to be different in the values we uphold and cherish. In a society which tells you that status, success and the freedom to do what you want are the things that matter, we dare to disagree. When governments believe they can create prosperity by neglecting the poor, we beg to differ.

We believe that all people are to be included in the boundless community. We believe that justice, mercy, truth and compassion are the standards by which the world ought to live. We are the sworn enemies of the grab-what-you-can philosophy. And that makes us different, or at least it ought to make us different, from a world which tells us to put 'me' at the heart of the universe.

So we say to (names of the parents) today – as we said to parents last week, and as we'll say to the parents who'll bring their child for baptism next week – your children will only believe this if they see it in you: they will only learn to care if they see how much you care; they will only put something ahead of their own interests if they see you trying to do the same.

What I need to say today is this: if we persist with this 'me first' society, it will lead to complete disintegration of community. That is the world your children and your grandchildren will grow up in. So what are you going to do to show there is another way?

What are you going to start giving to your community to help give us back our hope? For it is not the things we buy our children that shape their lives: it is the values we give them and the way we invite them to be partners in building a better world.

The poet Wordsworth put it best:

*What we have loved*
*others will love,*
*and we will teach them how.*

Colin McIntosh

## Blessing the water for baptism

Holy Spirit,
you moved over the waters
at the dawn of creation.
Bless this water
as we baptise *(name)* today.

Jesus Christ,
our master and our friend,
calling us to follow you.
Bless this water
as we baptise *(name)* into your church.

God our Maker,
thank you for the gift of life,
the chance to grow in your love.
Bless this water
as we baptise *(name)* into your family.

Chris Polhill


## Prayer over water

*As the water for baptism is poured:*

In waters of chaos and darkness,
in blood,
God's Spirit gives birth
to the things God makes good.

By the waters of heaven,
the flood from on high,
earth's evil was vanquished
as Noah found land
that was safe land and dry.

The Red Sea blew back
as God's people were fleeing
from slavery, hunger –
now it's us God is freeing!

The swift Jordan water
embraced God in Jesus;
the Spirit was gifted
as Jesus was lifted
and God's view was shifted:
his flesh and blood frees us.

So that *(name)*, who this day
is washed in this water,
may be made one with Christ in life, death and beyond.
Made new, made good, beloved of God.

Send your Holy Spirit to enfold *(name)* for new birth
in the family of your whole and holy church,
and raise *her/him* with Christ
to full and eternal life.
AMEN

David Coleman

## Oceans and puddles: a water litany

For oceans and puddles
THANK YOU GOD

For raindrops and fountains
THANK YOU GOD

For clean fresh water
THANK YOU GOD

For water stories in the Bible
THANK YOU GOD

For Moses in the bulrushes and Jonah and the big fish
THANK YOU GOD

For John the Baptist in the River Jordan
THANK YOU GOD

For Jesus in a boat and Peter in the water
THANK YOU GOD

For *(name)* brought here this morning
THANK YOU GOD

For *her/his* mum and dad and all *her/his* family
THANK YOU GOD

For all of us in the family of the church
THANK YOU GOD

God of water and wonder and new beginnings,
we bring you our thank yous and ourselves.
AMEN

Ruth Burgess


# A drop of water from the sea

A drop of water from the sea,
where all life began,
on your forehead, beloved,
to pour abundant life into you
all the days to come.

A drop of water from the sky,
bringing relief to the parched,
on your forehead, my beloved,
that your spirit
will never thirst for God's grace.

A drop of water from my heart,
overflowing with joy,
on your forehead, our beloved,
so you may feel God's hope
holding your hand
every faltering step you take.

One drop from the sea,
one drop from the sky,
one drop from my heart
mingle with Father, Son and Spirit,
the living waters
flowing with you forever,
beloved of God.
Amen

Thom M. Shuman

# Involving children at baptisms

When I do a formal baptism I get the youngest child who is old enough for the job to pour the water into the font. I tell them to listen to the prayer, and when I say the word 'water' to pour it in.

After I have anointed the baby with the sign of the cross, I invite the parents, godparents and any siblings to come and anoint the baby too.

Kes Grant

When I carry the newly baptised child around the church during the singing of a blessing, I encourage other children in the church to come and walk with me. This allows the adult congregation to sing the blessing to all the children present.

John L. Bell

# A naming and blessing story

I once took part in a naming and blessing ceremony where we passed around the circle a bell which the mother had worn during pregnancy, which therefore symbolised a connection with the child. People were asked to explain their connection to the child, and to offer their blessing. It was very moving.

Richard Sharples

# Practices from Friends

Quakers focus on the 'priesthood of all believers', and celebrate the sacramentality of all life. We have no formal baptism because we focus on the inner light in each of us, as we are 'baptised by the Holy Spirit' daily. But this doesn't mean we don't make a fuss about new children joining us, new friends becoming Friends.

Our girls were all welcomed to Quaker Meeting and have been active members of the Children's Meeting since then. On the first day that we brought them, babes in arms, to Meeting, at the end of the Meeting for Worship the oldest member took each child in her arms, stood and said: 'Friends, we welcome this new Friend amongst us in light and love.'

Here's a story from *Quaker Faith and Practice*:

*We were meeting in the long sitting-room and the floor-space was as usual filled by the children. The room was pretty full. Then Sophie's father came and put her carry-cot on the floor. She was very young, and we hadn't expected to be meeting her so soon. I looked around the adults, wondering which of us would minister.*

*At the other end of the room Cathy, aged three, slipped down from her mother's knee. Slowly, carefully, and mostly upright she clambered in and out, past all the other children. She reached the carry-cot and peeped in at the baby. Then she turned and gave everyone a smile of pure delight. Still smiling, without a word, she returned to her mother.*

Ruth Harvey

## Promises, from The Salvation Army

When a child is dedicated at a Salvation Army meeting the child's parents are asked, in the midst of the congregation, to make these promises:

*'In the dedication of this child you desire to give her/him fully to God. You wish to thank God for entrusting this precious life into your hands, and you want her/him to be nurtured in all that is pure, lovely and honest.*

*To this end you promise that you will keep from her/him, so far as you are able, everything which is likely to harm her/him in body, mind or spirit.*

*You also promise that, as she/he grows in wisdom and stature, you will teach her/him the truths of the gospel, encourage her/him to seek Christ as Saviour, and support her/him in the commitment of her/his life to the service of God.'*

Muriel Snell (Referenced from 'Guidance issued to officers of The Salvation Army')

## Baptism of a young boy and his baby sister

*A: young boy*

*B: baby sister*

A, before the world knew anything about you – before your mum and dad held you or first made you smile, before your aunts and uncles and grandparents sang you songs and pulled their silliest faces at you – God loved you. Before you made your first sounds, God looked forward to what you'd have to say; and before you took your first step, God was dreaming about the places you'd discover. For all your life, God's love and Christ's need will be mirrored in the eyes of the people you meet and the lives you touch. Today, we reach out and hand you what has been yours from the beginning: A, God's love is yours. Baptism is just our way of celebrating what already is.

A, I baptise you in the name of the Father, the Son and the Holy Spirit. May God's love and peace be with you now, and dwell in your heart forever ...

B, how can you know that there is a God who loves you so much that that love is mirrored in the eyes of your mum and dad – who couldn't imagine life without you? Minutes after you were born they placed you in the arms of your big brother *(name)*, standing right next to you, even now your protector – be sure, he will teach you, and argue with you, and make lots of noise and nonsense with you every day.

And how can you know that there are arms to hold you, minds to teach you, spirits to sing with yours? How can you know? You can't yet, but we're here to make sure that, in time, you'll come to know these things. B, you're loved because you come from God, who is love itself. And you belong to Jesus Christ, who calls us to freedom.

B, I baptise you in the name of the Father, the Son and the Holy Spirit. May God's love and peace be with you now, and dwell in your heart forever ...

Song: 'The Lord bless you and keep you'

Sally Foster-Fulton

# Some very important questions

*Leader (to all the children present at the service):*

*(Child's name)* is the newest member of the church. She is now part of your family. So each one of you is a brother or a sister to her.

Now I want to ask you some very important questions: When she falls down, will you help her up? When she's sad, will you give her a hug? When she is being a pain – like all of us are some of the time – will you love her anyway?

Will you listen to her, and will you tell her all the stories about Jesus that you've learned so that she can come to know them for herself?

If you will be there for *(child's name)*, say 'We will'.

*Children:*

We will.

Sally Foster-Fulton

## Baptism hymn

*(Tune: St Columba)*

We bring this child to church today
in joy and thankfulness,
as we in faith, on *his/her* behalf,
our solemn vows confess.

Enfolded in God's boundless love
this precious gift so small
is blessed with all the grace of God
by Christ who welcomes all.

We pray God's Spirit fill *his/her* life,
with love, joy, peace and light,
that *he/she* may grow encircled and
protected in God's sight.

In sign and symbol, praise and prayer
and set on Christ's new Way,
we place *him/her* now in God's embrace
for this and every day.

Carol Dixon and Stuart Brock

## A blessing for a baby born in spring

Welcome *(name)*:
You arrived with the greening leaves,
soft and delicate and strong,
unfolding into beauty and life.

Welcome *(name)*:
May your life be blessed with warmth and courage.
May the angels sing to you and the saints tell you stories.
May the Star-maker cradle you,
the Carpenter challenge you,
the Spirit safeguard you with laughter and love.

Welcome *(name)*:
May you bring joy to all who meet you.
May you grow each day in grace and wisdom.
May you dance in the sun and the rain and the wonder of God.

Ruth Burgess

## A blessing for a baby born in autumn

Welcome *(name)*:
you arrived with the beauty of tumbling leaves,
with the glory of harvest,
with the mystery of mist and the patter of rain.

Welcome *(name)*:
May your life be blessed with colour and wonder.
May the angels sing to you and the saints tell you stories.
May the Star-maker cradle you,
the Carpenter challenge you,
the Spirit safeguard you with laughter and love.

Welcome *(name)*:
May you bring joy to all who meet you.
May you grow each day in grace and wisdom.
May you dance in the leaves and the acorns and the wonder of God.

Ruth Burgess

## A blessing for a baby born in winter

Welcome *(name)*:
born into clear winter skies
with frost sparkling hard on the ground.

Welcome *(name)*:
May your life unfold in hope and adventure.
May the angels sing to you and the saints tell you stories.
May the Star-maker cradle you,
the Carpenter challenge you,
the Spirit safeguard you with laughter and love.

Welcome *(name)*:
May you bring joy to all who meet you.
May you grow each day in grace and wisdom.
May you dance in the snow and the starlight and the wonder of God.

Ruth Burgess

*\* Note: 'A blessing for a baby born in summer' can be found on p43*

# A dandling blessing *

*Isaiah 66:10–14*

When you are happy,
when you are full of life,
MAY GOD DANDLE YOU WITH LOVE.

When you are sad,
when you are full of tiredness,
MAY GOD CRADLE YOU WITH LOVE.

When you are growing,
when you are full of questions,
MAY GOD NURTURE YOU WITH LOVE.

All of your moments,
all of your nights and days,
MAY GOD DELIGHT IN YOU.
MAY GOD CHERISH YOU.
MAY YOU BE DANCED ON GOD'S KNEES
AND HELD IN GOD'S ARMS
WITH LOVE.

Ruth Burgess

*\*Dandle: 'to dance a child on one's knees, or in one's arms'* (Oxford Concise English Dictionary)

## For the gift of this child

For the gift of this child,
whose innocence and laughter keeps the world young,
we rejoice and give thanks.
May this new life,
which we have accepted into our community of ideals and friendship,
receive abundantly the blessings of health, love, knowledge and wisdom,
and in *(her/his)* turn give back these things richly.

And for the gift of parenthood we also give our thanks.
May all parents everywhere give their children security, freedom and love,
and may they be blessed with much joy,
much laughter
and much patience
in the divine task of nurture.
Amen

Kes Grant


## A baptismal moment (for Juan Diego)

May we too learn once again
how to be held in God's love
at each moment of our lives:
to lead with our hearts,
to show joy and tears
and be bathed in love.

As I hold you in my arms
I give thanks for your tiny life,
which calls forth from me
a love so deep that I feel
in holding you
I am held in God's embrace.

Fiona van Wissen

## Give us a swing, Jesus

A little kid ran across the street
runny-nosed – a bit scruffy,
tripping over almost.
She ran towards a man whose
arms were open wide to
welcome her.

'Give us a swing, Jesus,' she said,
and she felt herself lifted high –
and she saw the street and the sky whirling
around her – ablaze with colour –
like a mixed-up rainbow.
She was laughing then –
excited – free –
gasping for breath.
'Enough!' she said
and she felt herself slowing down
relaxing – safe –
as Jesus held her in his arms
and smiled.

Unless we become like
little children.
Unless we risk that joy
and abandonment.

Unless we run and ask
and let ourselves
be lifted high.

We are never going to
enter the Kingdom of God.

Ruth Burgess

## I long to dance

I long
I long to dance in the Spirit
just like a child
in the rain
on a summer's day;

I long
to slurp up
the living waters
the way my dog
empties his bowl
after a long walk;

I long
to stand
waist-deep
in the baptismal bowl
and feel
your tears of grace
wash over me;

I long
to hear
you call me
'Beloved'
and know –
beyond any doubt –
that is my name.

I long …

Thom M. Shuman

## An invitation to baptism

Splash!
It's time to get wet
Wet through
Soaked
Drenched
Sopping
Dripping
Saturated
Sodden
Drowned.

Splash!
That's what's going to happen.
And it's going to happen to you.

Splash!
This is what you've prayed about.
This is what God's called you to.
This is what you've asked for.
This is what you want to do.

Splash!
And it's a public splashing.
Everyone will be watching what's happening to you –
especially God!

Splash!
It's time to get wet:
wet through with Jesus
soaked with laughter
drenched with justice
sopping with loving
dripping with wonder
saturated with the Holy Spirit
sodden with mystery
drowned and raised to life in God.

Welcome to God's family.
Come and get wet!

Ruth Burgess

## Baptism blues (for Alice, my god-daughter)

Marimba

Pat Livingstone

Walked to my church to- day.  It was  a  hap-py day!

Laugh- ing,    talk- ing,    smi- ling,   pray- ing,   sing- ing.

Splish-splash this spe-cial day. God's child- ren now we pray.

Thank you,    God, you    love us    al - ways.    A- men.

Walked to my church today.
It was a happy day!
Laughing, talking, smiling, praying, singing.
Splish-splash this special day.
God's children now we pray.
Thank you, God, you love us always.
Amen

Pat Livingstone

Note:   I wrote 'Baptism blues' for my god-daughter Alice, who is five. She plays a
marimba/glockenspiel. She is still learning the notes so I printed the notes as
well as the letter names to enable her to play at her baptism.

Her sister, Rebecca, who is seven, plays the piano, and I wrote 'Baptism bells'
(p88) for her to play at her baptism.

Pat Livingstone, 2010

## Baptism bells (for Rebecca)

Piano

Pat Livingstone

## A prayer at baptism

Today we have stood with you
as you entered the waters of baptism,
your faith in Jesus expressed
as you surrendered yourself to him.

Today we have welcomed you
as you came up from the waters of baptism,
made new by the grace of God
and ready to follow the call of Christ.

Today we have received you
as you celebrated being a child of God,
and with joy we greeted you
as our *brother/sister* in Christ.

May God help you to be strong in your faith:
may your love for God deepen and grow.

May God reassure you of his love for you,
help you to discover the gifts you have
and grant you the confidence to use them.

May God guide you in the way you should go
that you may continue in the way of Christ.

May God help us to encourage you in your faith
and surround you with love.

And may God watch over you always
and keep you in his care,
fill you with his peace
and nurture you as his beloved child.

Simon Taylor

# John the Baptist

*(Matthew 3:1–12)*

People don't come to you by chance, John.
No one walks into the desert by accident:
you go there when you are driven,
you go there when you must –
when the choices have gone.

'Repent.
Turn around.
Change.
You are here knowing that God is angry with you;
you are here empty-handed;
you are here not knowing what will happen next.
Your good deeds cannot save you.
I cannot save you either.
This is only water,
water to show that you want to change,
that you want to be clean.
After me comes the one
who knows what you're like,
who will burn up the rubbish with fire.'

Not an easy preacher, John.
Would you have gone to hear him?
Would you have walked into the water?

*Discuss …*

Ruth Burgess

# Heard about?

*This script should be read by two 7-12-year-olds.*

*Mark 10:13–16*

Heard about the bust-up?

*Bust-up?*

Yeah – bust-up – it was great!

*Who was it?*

No one you'd have ever guessed.

*Stop kidding – who was it?*

Jesus!

*Jesus?*

Yeah, Jesus and his disciples and – a load of mums!

*A load of mums?*

Yeah, and a few dads too … but they weren't half as fierce as the mums.

*What happened?*

Well, you know that there seems to be a lot of babies around at the moment.

*Yeah, I know what you mean, loads of babies and little kids – my baby brother's one of them.*

Well, it seems that all the mums have taken a shine to Jesus … and they decided that, as Jesus is a kind of rabbi, they'd ask him to bless their children.

*Well, I can't see any problem with that – Jesus likes children.*

Ah – but the problem was that Jesus was busy doing something and the mums ran into the disciples.

*And? …*

And the disciples told the mums that Jesus was too busy to see them and …

*And? …*

And one of the disciples told the mums to go back home – and to take their noisy babies with them!

*He didn't!*

He did! Well, the mums were getting ready to sort this disciple out when Jesus appeared – and he was really cross.

*Cross with the mums?*

No!

*Cross with the babies?*

No!

*Cross with the disciples?*

Right third time!

*What did Jesus do?*

He told the disciples to let the mums bring the babies and children to him …

*And?*

And he took each child in his arms, or on his knee, and gave them a cuddle and said a wee blessing prayer.

*Bet the mums were pleased.*

Yeah, they were.

*You said there were some dads there too.*

There were, but I think that they'd decided to let the mums sort things out on their own, so they just watched … and smiled.

*So nobody really got hurt?*

Well, no, not really – but it was a great bust-up! And …

*And?*

And do you know what Jesus said?

*No, what?*

He said that children sometimes understand more about God's Kingdom than the grown-ups do …

*Cool. Must tell my big brother that.*

Better not, there might be a real bust-up!

Ruth Burgess

## Cwtch up, Cariad (a Welsh blessing)*

*Cwtch up, Cariad*
God's blessing is upon you

*Cwtch up, Cariad*
Jesus knows your name

*Cwtch up, Cariad*
The Holy Spirit watches over you

*Cwtch up, Cariad*
You're in a safe, safe place.

Ruth Burgess

*\* Cwtch: Cuddle, snuggle, love, protect, claim …*

*Cariad: 'Darling', 'Love', 'Beloved' …*

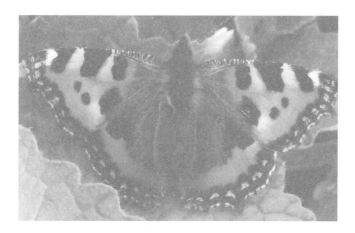

# Cradle roll service

*Before the service an invitation is sent to children who have been baptised in the church over the last 12 months and their families.*

**Opening activity:**

On entering the church the congregation are asked to write down one hope they have for their children (their natural children or any other children they have a particular concern for).

**Call to worship:**

Little people – little feet mean we have to slow down sometimes if we want to walk beside them. Little hands mean we have to help them do new things. Little attention spans and a giant energy source mean we have to learn the art of patience. They've only been on the planet for a little while but the future of the planet rests in their hands. Wait and walk and work beside them.

WE CAN SHOW EACH OTHER THE WAY.

Children – blink and they've grown. You look once and they're babies, turn for an instant and they're all arms and legs. Before you know it they're all attitudes and moods. Then whoosh – grown up and gone. Time flies by so don't waste a moment, unless you while away a day with them. Wait and walk and work beside them.

WE CAN SHOW EACH OTHER THE WAY.

Children – they don't have the experience to know the stuff we do: that discretion is the better part of valour, that silence is golden, that there are the ones who count, and the ones who don't. And they can help us unlearn these things if we let them. They have as much to teach us as we have to teach them. It's a win-win situation if I ever saw one! We're a match made in heaven! Take the time to discover each other. Wait and walk and work beside them.

WE CAN SHOW EACH OTHER THE WAY.

**Prayer** (*based on the hopes for children written down at the start of the service*)

**Bible reading**

**Hymn** (Says Jesus, 'Come and gather round', CH4 342)

**Story** (based on the reading)

Short reflection

Act of blessing:

*Parents and their children gather centrally and the congregation stand around them.*

*The promises of parents:*

In response to God's love for you, and in God's presence always, will you as parents strive to share your love, faith, understanding and forgiveness with your children, and, with God's help, make for them a home where they may learn to live in harmony and peace? Will you bless each other with the gifts you have to share?

*Parents:*

We will.

*The promises of the church:*

Will you all, who form the community in which our children live, keep these children and their parents in your hearts and prayers, and, with God's help, be an example of faith, hope and love to them? Will you bless each other with the gifts you have to share?

*Parents:*

We will.

*Parents hold their children and together with the congregation pray:*

OUR CHILDREN,
MAY GOD'S JOY BE IN YOUR HEARTS
AND GOD'S LOVE SURROUND YOUR LIVING,
EACH DAY AND NIGHT
AND WHEREVER YOU ROAM.
MAY YOU KNOW GOD'S PRESENCE
IN GROWING AND LEARNING,
IN JOYS AND SORROWS,
IN FRIENDSHIP,
IN SOLITUDE,
IN BEGINNINGS AND ENDINGS.
MAY GOD KEEP AND BLESS YOU
ALL THE DAYS OF YOUR LIVES. AMEN

*Parents and children return to their seats.*

Final hymn ('You shall go out with joy', CH4 804)

**Benediction:**

This is your home.
Come when you can.
The door will always be open.

Beloved of God,
and that's who you are,
go in peace,
and the blessing of God, Father, Son and Holy Spirit,
be with you today and every day. Amen

Sally Foster-Fulton and Colin McIntosh

# Liturgies of baptism for older children and adults

# Baptism of older children

*This can be adapted for use in Mass. It was originally used for the baptism of children, but could be adapted for adult baptism.*

*Those to be baptised are at the back of the church/room with their godparents.*

*The leader (priest or deacon) welcomes those gathered.*

Opening responses:

My dear brothers and sisters,
as children of the living God, we rejoice when others come to us
and ask to become part of the worldwide family of God.

Today *(names of children)* are taking the great step
of being baptised into our Church.
They become part of a story that goes back thousands of years.
They become part of the great people of God
spread throughout the world.
They become the brothers and sisters of people in countries far away –
but it is the community here in *(place)*
which has the privilege of welcoming them
and gathering them into the family of God.

My sisters and brothers, *(names of children)*
are waiting for our invitation to them to come into our community
and be baptised into the life and love of God.

*(NAMES OF CHILDREN),*
WE ARE PROUD THAT YOU WANT TO BECOME
PART OF OUR COMMUNITY OF FAITH.
WE WELCOME YOU WITH OPEN ARMS.
WE INVITE YOU TO COME TO THE ALTAR
AND TO BE BAPTISED INTO THE LIFE AND LOVE OF GOD.

WE RECEIVE YOU AS PEOPLE WHO HAVE HEARD THE CALL OF JESUS
AND WHO ARE READY TO BECOME SONS AND DAUGHTERS OF GOD.

WE REJOICE IN THE GREAT THINGS THAT GOD HAS DONE FOR YOU
AND WILL DO FOR YOU.

*(NAMES OF CHILDREN),* WE WELCOME YOU:
IN THE NAME OF THE FATHER, THE SON AND THE HOLY SPIRIT.

*Those to be baptised come forward, while simple background music is played.*

Scripture reading(s)

Receiving the symbols of baptism:

In our tradition we use symbols and signs to help us show what God is doing.

Today, we have asked *(names of children),* who have already been baptised, to bring forward the symbols of baptism for *(name of children)* for us to reflect on.

*A cross is brought forward.*

On Good Friday, Jesus died on the cross for us. But this was not the end of the story, for Jesus was raised from the dead. The cross is not a symbol of death but of life.

*Oil is brought forward.*

Oil is used to anoint kings and queens. Jesus, our King, was raised from the dead. We are made special in baptism by the oil of chrism.

*A jug of water is brought forward.*

Plants, animals and people need water. Without water we die. Water is a sign of life. In baptism we share in Jesus' New Life.

*White garments are brought forward.*

Today we celebrate Jesus' New Life – we are all made new in Jesus. These white garments are a symbol of our New Life.

*Three candles are brought forward.*

On Good Friday everything went dark – but today the light of Christ shines everywhere. At our baptism we receive the light of Christ.

We have welcomed *(names of children)* and prepare to baptise them.

Let us now proclaim for them the faith which we are proud to profess.

Renewal of baptismal promises

Baptismal promises:

*Leader:*

*(Names of children),* you have heard all these people proclaim what they believe about

being a Christian. Now it is your turn to tell us what you have learnt.

*(Names of children)*, do you believe that God loves you very much and wants you to be part of his Christian family?

*Children:*

Yes.

*Leader:*

Do you believe that Jesus Christ is the Son of God, that he came into the world to show us how to live a life of love, and died so that we could live forever?

*Children:*

Yes.

*Leader:*

Do you believe in the Holy Spirit, who will live in your heart and help you to grow in goodness and to make good choices as you grow older?

*Children:*

Yes.

*Leader:*

Do you believe that the Church is God's family in the world, a great family that is spread through the earth?

*Children:*

Yes.

*Leader:*

Do you believe that you are very special to God: that God knows your names and has written them on the palms of his hands? Do you promise to do your best to live as God wants you to: being kind, loving and generous, and strong and not afraid to be a Christian?

*Children:*

Yes.

*Parents and godparents are asked to give consent.*

*Leader:*

Parents and godparents, you have heard *(names of children)* express their desire to be baptised and to become part of the family of God. Do you give your consent to their being baptised?

*Parents and godparents:*

We do.

*Leader:*

Are you willing to cherish the simple faith that *(names of children)* have expressed and to help it grow to maturity in the years ahead?

*Parents and godparents:*

We are.

*Leader:*

Are you willing to support them and encourage them when they begin to face questions and doubts; when being young men and women of faith becomes a challenge, rather than a simple joy?

*Parents and godparents:*

We are.

*Leader:*

*(Names of children)*, your parents have given their consent to your being baptised, so, on behalf of this community at *(place/church)*, I am delighted to welcome you and to baptise you into our life of faith.

Baptism

Giving of candles:

*Leader:*

Parents and godparents, these lights are lit from the paschal candle, our sign of the risen Christ alive in the world today. I ask you to receive this light and to pass it on to your children: as a sign of your willingness to guard and protect the light of faith that is in them.

*Candles are handed to parents and godparents, who hand them on to the children.*

*If this service is used in Mass, Mass continues. The newly baptised children can bring up the gifts.*

**Closing responses:**

We have welcomed *(names of children)* into our community of faith.
WE REJOICE WITH THEM, WITH THEIR FAMILIES AND WITH THEIR FRIENDS.

We pray that their lives will be happy
and filled with the great things that God has promised to his children.
May they walk tall and proud as children of the living God.
ALLELUIA!

We have remembered that we too have been chosen
and welcomed into the community of faith.
WE RENEW OUR FAITH AND GO ON OUR WAY TO LIVE, TO LOVE
AND TO TELL THE GOOD NEWS THAT JESUS CHRIST IS LORD!
ALLELUIA!

Wellspring

# Liturgy of baptism

**Welcome**

**Call to worship**

**Song**

**Prayer of approach, confession and assurance of pardon:**

Holy God, we thank you for all things bright and beautiful – for you bless us with such an amazing world. You bless us with friends and family – a wonderful variety of people – and with breathtaking scenery around us. Help us to appreciate the wonder and beauty, to enjoy and not be cynical or despairing, to appreciate each precious moment and live fully in the moment, not harking back to what was, or rushing forward to an unknown and unknowable future.

To serve you we need to be completely honest and bring to you all that we are.

In order to be open to the gift of your grace we need to let go of all that shuts us off from the wonder of your love.

So we bring to you now all that stops us living fully in joy and peace and wonder ...

Turn us round to your new way of living. Help us to forgive others, to forgive ourselves, for if we are ready to change, you forgive us.

So take us, challenge us, renew us. It is not who we were that is important, but who we *are* and who we *can be* with you, starting now.

Thanks be to God.

Lord's Prayer

Song

*Introduce the one to be baptised (A).*

The liturgy of baptism:

What is baptism for?

What was God doing in becoming one of us in Jesus? God was showing the immense love that is with us, for God loves us so much that he was prepared to be born as one of us: God Almighty became God the vulnerable.

When John the Baptist was baptising people in need of change, Jesus, who had nothing to put right, came to be baptised in the River Jordan to be alongside people like us. When Jesus came up out of the water – the sky burst open, and the Holy Spirit came down upon him in the form of a dove. And a voice from heaven said: 'You are my own dear child, and I am pleased with you.'

Jesus, the child God, the parent God, and God the Holy Spirit are present in baptism. The Holy Spirit was given to the Church at Pentecost, when everyone who put their trust in Jesus began to speak out in whatever way was needed, to get through all the walls people build up against each other and to keep God out.

We are the same community gathered here today, commanded to make new disciples by baptising and teaching.

Teaching everything that has been shown us by Christ, both in his human lifetime and beyond; baptising with water, into the midst of God: into the name of the Father, the Son and the Holy Spirit, the Mother of us all, who is God as Jesus showed us.

The God that our life together should always reflect.

And so we declare our faith.

Statement of faith:

WE BELIEVE IN A GOD OF RAINBOWS,
WHO CREATES ALL THROUGH LOVE.
WHO PROMISES TO BE WITH CREATION:
IN SUN AND RAIN,
IN JOY AND PAIN.
WHO BLESSES US WITH WONDER IN EACH MOMENT
AND JOY IN EACH STEP.

WE BELIEVE IN GOD WHO LOVES US
AND BECOMES ONE WITH US IN JESUS.
WHO, IN SOLIDARITY, SUFFERS WITH US.
WHO KNEW DESPAIR AND LOSS AND BETRAYAL.
WHO WAS KILLED FOR STANDING UP FOR WHAT IS RIGHT,
YET WHO SHOWED THAT LOVE IS STRONGER THAN DEATH.

WE BELIEVE IN GOD.
WHO IS GIFTED TO US IN THE SPIRIT.
WHO ENFOLDS AND UPHOLDS US.
WHO INSPIRES US WITH THE VISION OF HOW THINGS SHOULD BE.
WHO CHALLENGES US TO LIVE HONESTLY.
WHO TRANSFORMS OUR PAIN INTO NEW LIFE.
WHO EMPOWERS US WITH NEW BEGINNINGS.
WE BELIEVE IN A GOD OF LOVE AND LAUGHTER
WHO CALLS US TO LIVE TODAY IN JUSTICE AND JOY,
BUILDING COMMUNITIES OF UNITY AND PEACE.

*Invite A and sponsor to come forward.*

Confession of faith:

*Leader:*

You have come in response to the call of Christ
and the leading of the Holy Spirit
to be baptised.
Let us hear from you that you confess your faith in Christ.

*A:*

I believe and trust in one God,
Father, Son and Holy Spirit,
Maker of heaven and earth,
Giver of life, Redeemer of the world.

*The water is poured into the font.*

Prayer over the water:

Blessed are you, Lord God of all creation.
In your goodness you give us water
to sustain our life and renew the earth.
BLESSED BE GOD FOREVER.

God in the beginning, over the water,
calling forth light and life and loveliness;
leading your people, unharmed by the waters,
from slavery to freedom in a land of promise.
Releasing the Spirit to Jesus in the river.

Then from Jesus sprang
the water of life for all the world.
Though killed by those who feared what he offered,
Christ burst out from the grave
to shower us with new and unlimited life.

Send your Holy Spirit upon us and upon this water, that A,
born anew of water and the Spirit,
may remain forever in the number of your faithful people,
through Jesus Christ our Lord.
In the name of God our Source, Word and Liberating Spirit
to whom be all honour and glory, now and forever.
AMEN

The baptism:

*Leader:*

I baptise you in the name of the Father, the Son and the Holy Spirit. Amen

**Signing of the cross with oil:**

*Leader:*

I mark you with the sign of the cross: the sign of Christ, the sign of heaven in solidarity with earth.

**Lighting the candle:**

*Leader:*

I give you this candle that you may shine as a light in the world for Christ, who is our Light. Your baptism is a sign of your commitment to shine with God's love. Receive this light.

**Declaration of baptism:**

And so, A, God receives you by baptism into the one holy, catholic and apostolic Church. May the Lord bless you and keep you.

**Blessing (spoken or sung)**

**The promises:**

A belongs to God in Christ. God has done God's part.

So we make our promises:

*Promises by sponsor:*

Do you *(name of sponsor)*, A's sponsor, promise to show *her/him* God's love? Do you promise to offer care and encouragement, nurturing *her/him* in body, mind and spirit to live a life of faith and justice, supporting *her/him* in *her/his* spiritual journey?

*Sponsor:*

I do.

*Promises by the elders:*

Do you promise to pray for A, and to support *her/him* as you are able, as ministers of Christ's love?

*Elders:*

We do.

*Invite all to stand.*

*Promise by the congregation:*

*Leader:*

Do you promise to share the gifts of God's grace with A, nurturing *her/him* with your joy, your questions, your faith and your love and supporting *her/him* in *her/his* spiritual journey?

WITH GOD'S HELP, WE DO.

*Music is played as A meets the congregation.*

**Presentation of certificate and a Bible**

**Welcome:**

IN THE NAME OF CHRIST WE WELCOME YOU *(NAME)*.
MAY WE GROW TOGETHER IN UNITY,
AND BE BUILT UP INTO THE BODY OF CHRIST IN LOVE,
TO THE GLORY OF GOD,
FATHER, SON AND HOLY SPIRIT,
NOW AND FOREVER.
AMEN

Zam Walker

# Parenthood and grandparenthood

## Prayer for parents and for those who wish to be parents

*Use two voices*

We pray …

for those who got pregnant right away, and for those who have been trying for years …

*For those who can't wait to welcome a baby into their home, and for those who are terrified that they are not fit to be parents …*

For those whose child will get a football scholarship, and for those whose child will never run …

*For those who pose proudly for photos pregnant with possibility, and for those who shamefully hide their bellies …*

For those who are proud to be fathers, and for those who hope the DNA test will not match …

*For those who pay child support, and for those who need child support …*

For those who fight with teenage daughters, and for those whose daughters have run away from home …

*For those who cannot pay for college, and for those who cannot pay for medical care …*

For those who homeschool, and for those who fear their children won't make it home from school …

*For those whose children are in prison, and for those whose children want to be prison chaplains …*

For those whose baby doesn't live outside of the womb, and for those whose wombs are empty …

*For those taking hormone treatment, and for those who feel exhausted from hormone changes …*

For those grieving what will never be, and for those amazed by what life has become …

*For those who are single parents, and for those who are now step-parents …*

For those who have an empty nest, and for those whose nest was never full …

*For the couple who feel closer than ever, and for the couple getting divorced …*

For all of your children of all ages:

*Hold them close, God, and give them life.*

Amen

Ashley-Anne Masters


## Praise God for a granddaughter

Praise God for a granddaughter.
For happily playing the same simple games
over and over again.
For being pleased to sing the same silly songs
for hours.
For delight in seeing a flower, a dog, a frog …

Thank you, Lord, for teaching me to become like a little child
and helping me enter the kingdom of heaven.

Brian Ford


## Thanksgiving for a child

We thank you, Lord, for the gift of our child
and for all the joy and love she has brought into our lives.
We thank you for precious moments together
and the delight of sharing our life with another.

We thank you for her bright smile,
for her playfulness and sense of fun;
for all the love and affection she gives;
for her curiosity and wish to explore.
We learn so much from her openness
and her willingness to trust.

We thank you, Lord, for all the ways in which she touches our lives:
we treasure our child and the memories we are being given.
We thank you for all those who help and support us as a family:
for grans and granddads, uncles and aunts,
for friends and teachers, doctors and nurses.

And as our beloved child grows
help us not to cling to her so tightly
that she cannot find the space to express her own creativity and will.

Help us to let her go when the time is right
that she may walk her own road
and freely return the love she has been given.

And we ask you, loving God,
who is mother and father to all,
that you would always hold her in your loving arms
and surround her with your peace.
And that you will always be there to guide her along the way.

Simon Taylor


## Raising kids

Not much of a job raising kids, some folk may say –
when kids are tiny and you go to bed whacked
and they scream through the night, leaking at both ends,
night after night, night after night.

As children grow, not knowing how much rope to let out, scared,
we restrict their independence
or unfairly give them too much rope.

And in adolescence, baffled about how to encourage sexual integrity,
we're relieved that we need not only do our best
but can place them in your hands through prayer,
and call on the resources of the Holy Spirit.

Come to our help, Lord God:
make the impossible possible.

Ian M. Fraser

## Matthew's hug

There is a rustle at the door,
footsteps bound across the room,
arms are flung round me.

And in that instant
there is total acceptance,
love
unconditional,
no need for words.
Just to be
together,
giving and receiving,
holding on tight,
not wanting the moment to end.

And there is God.

But the little body becomes restless,
struggles to be free.
I release my hold
and watch him run,
and turn,
and smile,
'I love you, Mummy.'

And there is God.

Julia Brown

## How am I supposed to pray?

How am I supposed to pray
with this racket going on?
Don't you realise I have to talk to my Maker
about important things
you know nothing of?

How am I supposed to pray
with you jumping all over me?
Demanding attention,
affirmation as I pull the duvet from under you
to screams of delight.

How am I supposed to pray?
How would you know?
You have no religion, just the expectation of
being heard at any moment.

I love that about you.
And I hear you, my little teacher.
I hear you.

David McNeish

# School and growing up

## Blessing for those beginning school

You are beginning.

From here – things are going to get exciting.
You are going to school.
And this is your work:
to learn to be with others,
to wonder and to ask,
to explore,
to imagine and to share.

You are beginning.
So make friends – dare to ask someone's name.
Say who you are.
Take your place in school.
Learn about the world.

We will be here to help you when you need it.
We will be here to listen to your stories.
We want to know what it is like for you
because we remember.

And now it is you.

You are beginning.

Katie Munnik


## New school

I'm in a new school today,
I'll never know what to say.
Everyone's here or there.
Sometimes people even swear!
Everybody has their mates,
I'm just sitting there by the gates.
I really hope I'll get a 'bud'.
Someone just really should
just happen to come my way –
and ask if I'll come and play!

So here I am on my tod.
But I have someone to talk to,
and that's God.

Annie Sharples, aged 12


## Blessing for a new school term

Loving God, we ask you to be with us in this new term.

Be with our teachers and teaching assistants as they help us learn,
be with those who look after our school
and be with us as we gather here each week.
Help us to listen to each other
and to care for one another.
May we enjoy our learning and our playing
and discover more of this wonderful world we share.
Make us better friends
and concerned when someone is sad.

Loving God,
bless our school with your love,
with your kindness,
with your peace.
Amen

Simon Taylor

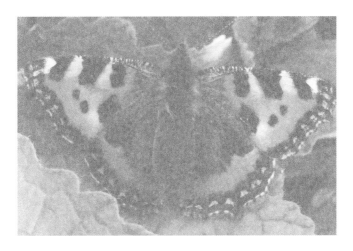

## The school playground: memoir of a postwar London-Irish childhood

My early childhood was lived in central London, where I attended a small convent primary school close to Marylebone High Street and the Spanish Place Church.

The convent and school were housed in a tall imposing Victorian building surrounded by high railings. The juniors had their playground on the roof of the building. The infants played in the yard, which was an area enclosed on all four sides by ugly, prison-like brick walls.

At one end of the yard were the toilets. Smelly places with wooden doors that didn't lock and cisterns that flushed inadequately.

At the opposite end of the yard were strong iron railings that prevented children from falling down into the basement, where food was prepared and from which the smell of stew and cabbage would drift up and across the playground.

The yard was entered from the school hall and the 'dinner lady' – a big-boned woman with tightly bound, brown permed hair – would stand on guard at the doorway, her arms folded, whilst she glared menacingly at the children. Periodically she would bellow punitive warnings at the boys who indulged in brawls, rolling around on the ground, kicking and dragging at one another's clothes and limbs. Other boys raced around the yard with arms outstretched, screaming and roaring in their fantasies of wartime aeroplanes and bombs.

The girls played quieter games and were more communal. 'Mothers and fathers', in which the drama was meticulously planned first of all. Some played singing games: 'In and out the dusty bluebells', or 'Donkey', where a ball was thrown against a wall and jumped over as it bounced on the ground. Some practised their Irish dancing, or did handstands up against the wall, tucking their gymslips into the elasticated legs of their thick navy-blue knickers.

Sometimes I would stand alone, hating the noise and the smells and the claustrophobic yard where you had to bend your neck back and look vertically upwards to see the clouds and the sky.

Often I would escape from the cacophony by asking permission to pray in the convent chapel. I loved the chapel, with its cream walls and highly polished wooden floor. There was always a nun at the back, lost in prayer and snoring gently. I was comforted by her presence, feeling her to be a kindred spirit in this silent world of candles and flowers surrounding a huge ornate, golden monstrance, which enclosed in its window a pure white Host.

The noise from the playground drifted monotonously through the high chapel windows that looked onto the yard. But sitting in one of the wooden pews I would close my eyes and allow myself to forget the concrete playground with its invasive noise and smells, and enter, instead, the other world of my childhood …

I was in the kitchen of my Irish grandparents' farmhouse in County Mayo. My grandmother had cut me a large slice of bread made with dried fruit and covered it with thick homemade jam. Taking this, I went out through the back door, pausing in the yard to share my feast with the ever-hopeful hens, and then along the mud path, past the hen house on the left, with its rhubarb patch and blackberries, and the cowshed on the right. Past the apple trees, but leaving the path to wind its way to the well, and going instead diagonally across the field that rose gradually on the side of the hill. I scrambled over the dry-stone wall and crossed the next field, slightly steeper now as it neared the summit of the hill. This was my favourite field, and in it I had a special corner where I would sit and munch the warm homemade bread that my grandmother had given me. I would look across the fields to the misty curves of the distant blue hills and wonder what secrets they held. Stretched out below was the flat bog. My grandparents called it the 'Far Land', and I would gaze across it, searching amongst the grazing cattle and working farmers for the figure of my uncle Ulick, cutting turf and loading it into the cart strapped to the patiently waiting long-eared ass.

Beyond the bog was the deserted road, making its way steadily towards Westport and the steep pyramid-shaped Croagh Patrick. I was in awe of this mountain that changed colour according to the time of day and the weather – green, blue, purple, grey. In early morning the scree would glow white in the sunlight, broken and worn evidence of the thousands of pilgrims who had reached its peak in barefooted penance.

I became engrossed in the silence this mountain imposed, sometimes watching the clouds that would rest mysteriously on its peak and hide it in a thick swirling mist.

Sitting on the grass in my sacred corner, I kept very still, feeling a gentle breeze, smelling the earth and its freshness. Sometimes frogs would leap through the wet grass, pausing a while to survey me and decide on the level of danger I might threaten to their customary activities.

Suddenly the background noise from the playground would cease and I would hear the dinner lady clanging the bell and yelling at the children. It was time to leave my hidden world and return to the concrete yard, joining my friends who would already be in lines waiting to be sent to the classrooms.

As I left the chapel the nun at the back would always give me a warm smile, almost as though she knew the secret of where I had been whilst sitting in the chapel pew.

June McAllister

## Bullies

There they go strutting about,
nearly always with a pout!
They always shout: 'Get out my way.
You had better do as I say!'
If we do one thing wrong –
they'll give our heads one big dong!
I'm really scared of that dude –
one day maybe he'll strip people nude!
But I've just got to think about it:
why they're like that, just one bit.
Maybe they got bullied in their day?
Possibly that's what God will say.

Annie Sharples, aged 12

## Sports day

When I was in Year 6 I was chosen to do the long jump and relay for the district Sports day. We had been practising for ages, so when the day came I was nervous and thought that I couldn't do it, but a little voice kept telling me: *'You* can *do it, and so what if you lose? Not that you will because you will do your best!'* It helped that I was with two friends and my little sister. Anyway, all of the team were supporting each other, which meant a lot to me.

At the sandpit there were taller girls with longer legs and a lot more practice. My legs were shaking each time I jumped – it was so scary! They announced the results ages later; in the meantime I had been shouting and cheering for all the others when they were racing! I had come 3rd – and I was chuffed to bits.

Next was the relay, and our team waited for our time. Again my legs were shaking. The gun went – and that's when I saw our whole school team, my dad and sister cheering us on!

When I started running I went for it, concentrating on number 4 on our team. I passed the baton to her and slipped. I was on the ground but she crossed the line. We came 3rd again – we heard a massive cheer!

At the end we were so happy. No, we didn't beat everyone but I didn't care. I was thanking God that it went so well, because he was watching me all the way through.

Mary Sharples, aged 11

## I wish

I wish I was a nurse
I wish I was a singer
I wish I could fly in a rocket
I wish I was a rich woman

I wish I was a pit bull terrier in case anybody burgled my mum's house
I wish I had a cottage by the sea
I wish I had some money to spend
I wish I had a garden

I wish I wasn't at school
I wish I wasn't working
I wish I was in bed
I wish I was a big girl

I wish that people were kind
I wish that nobody fights
I wish that nobody dies
I wish that Jesus was here

I wish I was a bird
I wish I had two cars
I wish I was a panther in the jungle
I wish I had a pot of gold

I wish I had 200,000 Mars Bars
I wish I was a dog sleeping beside a fire
I wish my mum had a baby
I wish I had lots of money to buy anything I like

I wish that I could go to Disneyland for three years
I wish that nobody steals from the shops
I wish that I was grown up
I wish that every day I could sit beside the fire with a cup of tea

I wish I was getting married to Louis
I wish I was the boss
I wish I had lots of paper
I wish I had a silver dream machine

A class of 7-year-olds

## A prayer for primary-school leavers

Dear Lord,
we thank you for our school,
for all that we have learnt here
and for all the new things we have found out.
We thank you for the friends we have made
and for the time to learn and play together.
We thank you for those who have taught us
and for all who care for our school.

We ask you to be with us in our new school:
help us to achieve our hopes and dreams,
help us to always be friends
and to continue to care for each other.

Thank you Lord for your love for us
and for your promise that,
wherever we may go,
you will be with us.
Amen

Simon Taylor

## A prayer for a test

*This is a prayer I say to myself at night when I have a science test the following day!*

Dear God,
I have a test tomorrow:
please help me to do my best.
And help me to know
if I do poorly
that you'll still love me
just as I am.

Please help me to remember
that you are always there beside me,
every second of the day.
Thank you, Lord.
Amen

Annie Sharples, aged 12

## Prayer at a Sunday school prize-giving service

Loving God,
in your great love for us
you have given us
all we need for life,
all we need to praise you,
all we need to serve our neighbours.

Gathered here today
as a family of your people,
we thank you for all these gifts.

And especially we thank you
for the work of the Christian Education Department
over this session which has ended,
for teachers and helpers,
for children and parents and grandparents,
and for the many families
represented in this congregation,
week by week.

We thank you, too, for our bodies.

For our feet,
on which we can step out
on the journey of life,
following Jesus.

For our hands,
with which we can make things,
and serve each other.

For our voices,
with which we can sing and shout your praises
and our love of life,
and tell your story to others.

We dedicate our bodies now –
feet, hands, voices –
and our whole lives to you.
In Jesus' name.

John Harvey

## Telling people about my religion

*This one was quite hard to write – it's about telling people that I go to church …*

'What do you do on Sunday?'
'Nothing much,' I'll usually say.
'Do you want to go to town?'
'Sorry,' I say with a frown.
'What's the matter?' On they go.
'Really nothing you should know.'
'Seriously, why can't you come then?'
'I've got church at half past ten!'

Annie Sharples, aged 12


## Laces

He looked me in the eye
and he asked me
'Can you do shoelaces?'

Tricky things, shoelaces,
particularly this one
which on examination
turned out to be in three pieces
knotted together
with all six ends fraying.

So we sat down in the gutter
and he took off his shoe.
And slowly I undid and did the shoelace,
and we threaded it carefully
through the right holes.

Then he put his shoe back on
and I finished the job
with a wonky bow.

He looked me in the eye again
and said,
'Thank you',

and we parted smiling,
each to carry on
with our respective days.

Ruth Burgess


## Prayer for school leavers

Today, as you take yet another step on your journey,
we want you to know that our love and admiration
and prayers surround you.

We offer our hands to hold yours,
our hearts to cheer yours,
and our feet to join you when you need us to walk with you.

We send prayers aloft that your lives will not offer what you expect exactly,
but that life will continually surprise you.

We pray that you will be used by the God who created you,
led by the Christ who teaches you
and challenged by the Spirit
who leads you on.

Sally Foster-Fulton

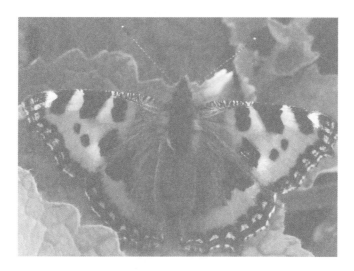

Teens

## Something more

*'Hey, hey, my, my,*
*rock 'n' roll can never die.*
*There's more to the picture*
*than meets the eye.*
*Hey, hey, my, my …'*
Neil Young

Home for lunch, you listened to music – like snatches of bread.

After school, you went up to your room, and listened to music.

When you went to bed at night, you listened to music, on your clock radio (set it so that you fell asleep before it suddenly went silent – and so that you woke up in the morning: listening to music).

On weekends we went to the great stadiums and halls, to worship our gods – Led Zeppelin, Pink Floyd, Bruce Springsteen …

Seeing Bruce at Cobo in Detroit one time, it was like 5000 people became One. Everyone knew all the words. During 'Born to Run', everyone held up their cigarette lighters, and when you glanced around it was like a sky full of stars. Like you were in heaven …

We went on pilgrimages:

One day took three buses and walked about 10 miles under the summer sun – shining and shimmering like a Zildjian symbol – to Steve's Music Store just to see, and actually touch, a guitar like the one Jimmy Page played on 'Stairway to Heaven', in the film *The Song Remains the Same* (which we'd seen at The Palace fifteen times) – a Gibson Les Paul with a double neck.

Woke up early Saturday mornings to be at Virgin Records the moment it opened (with coupons we'd cut out of the newspaper) – to be the very first in our high school to get our hands on the 'Album of the Week': *Rumours, The Wall, Ghost in the Machine* … The ritual was that we bought hangover coffee and donuts and went over to Joff's house to listen.

During more musically mature years, near the end of high school, skipped math class and drove downtown to 'Crazy Dave's Second Hand Record Store' – which was like a temple – with icons tacked and taped up everywhere: Dylan, The Clash, Jimi Hendrix … Goddesses: Patti Smith, Debbie Harry, Stevie Nicks, Joni. Crazy Dave had actually been to Woodstock, and to Altamont. He'd seen every band, had met the Stones – and once shared a joint with the high priest of rock 'n' roll, Keith Richards.

We spent entire afternoons searching through the tightly packed bins and crates for treasure, getting high on the opium-scented joss sticks Dave burned – on the heady incense of cardboard, glue and vinyl – and sometimes found gold: *Metal Machine Music* by Lou Reed. Or something you'd never heard of in your life – that opened up a whole exotic, strange new world: *Tales of Topographic Oceans* by Yes. Or that woke you up – finally – and brought you back down to earth – with a good slap: The Clash's first album, with 'White Riot' and 'Cops and Thieves' …

We got part-time jobs just to buy more albums, better stereo equipment and go to shows. You'd give ten million dollars to see the Beatles reunited.

One time, at a concert in Detroit, I actually got close enough to the stage to reach out and touch Neil Young, as he held his hand out over the crowd: the hand of the man who had written 'Heart of Gold', and had played the classic riff on 'Mr Soul'; and right after, my friends touched me, grabbed my hand, and held it, and other people around me too, brothers and sisters … For a moment I felt blessed, elect, healed …

Late one night, we held a solemn rite in which we barbecued all of Joff's sister's disco records: 'Burn, baby, burn, disco inferno,' we chanted, as they melted over the grill; flared and smoked evilly in the moonlight.

When John Lennon was shot and killed, we held a vigil in Joff's basement bedroom: Lit white candles and quietly sang 'Give Peace a Chance', 'Help', 'Strawberry Fields Forever' … (Joff was learning guitar.) It was the first time we ever hugged and saw each other cry …

In the movie *The Doors* (which we saw at The Palace ten times) Jim Morrison says shamanically to somebody: 'You think that, in the end, all people want is two cars and house? … Well, you're wrong … What they want is … *something sacred* …'

We never realised it then. It was instinctive. Our love of rock 'n' roll was the reaching out for something sacred. Something more than the long, flat, treeless Main Street paved with car plants, used-car lots, shopping malls full of musak, McDonald's, Kentucky Fried Chickens, Taco Bells, billboards of real estate agents with friendly mouths full of teeth …

Something more than a lifetime of jobs at the factory, and the repetitive deadening beat of the assembly line that made you a zomboid. Or the passionlessness, predictable, safe, shallow, monotonous rhythm, and glitter and polish, of a white-collar disco life.

We could never put it into words. It was more a feeling.

Walking home one summer night after an Ian Hunter and Mick Ronson concert – under a sky full of stars shining like a million BIC lighters – Joff and I tried.

Joff said: 'I don't why I love music so much. It just takes me away someplace else, you know?'

We talked about hearing a great song for the first time – and getting chills: the feeling of the hair on the back of your neck standing up on end with the electricity.

Or hearing something totally different and new on your car radio, and having to pull over to the side of the road to listen, while everyone else – the whole world – just passes by: stuck inside the machine, sleepwalking …

'Yeah! And that's how I want to experience and live my whole life!' I sang out, frustrated. 'With that same … passion.'

'Same awareness,' Joff answered.

'Yeah – yeah, yeah, yeah!'

'Soon as I can, I'm gettin' outta this town,' said Joff.

''Cause tramps like us, baby, we were born to run,' I sang.

'Exactly,' said Joff.

And we walked home together – singing at the tops of our lungs over dogs barking and someone, barricaded and asleep behind their white-picket-fence dream, shouting at us to be quiet! Guided home by the stars: the eternal souls of saints John, Jimi, Janis …

Neil Paynter

## When Jesus was a teenager

When Jesus was a twelve-year-old
he calmed his parents' fears.
He was a good, obedient boy,
but did he bring his mother joy
all through his teenage years?

When Jesus was a teenager
did he have spots like me?
A cracking voice and sprouting hair –
hormones all going everywhere!
How was his puberty?

When Jesus went to Rabbi school,
as every young Jew should,
he knew his scriptures inside out.
Did they, like now, begin to doubt?
'No one can be that good!'

When Jesus reached 'that awkward age'
did he have moods like mine?
And switch from joy to deep despair –
from larking about to full of care.
Did Jesus always shine?

When Jesus was a handsome lad
(the Son of God above),
did he have times he couldn't speak –
with racing pulse and blushing cheek?
Did Jesus fall in love?

When Jesus was a teenager
what did they often say?
'Now you're a man ...' It drives me wild,
for then they treat you like a child!
But still he found his Way.

Jesus, you were a teenager:
went through it all like me.
Please keep me strong, allay my fears.
Help me to journey through the years
to life that's full and free.

David Lemmon

## Prayer for those going to university

As you leave your home
and make this next step towards being self-reliant
we pray that all will go well for you.

May you be homesick enough to remember
how much those back home love and care for you,
but not so homesick that you cannot bear to be away from them.
May you like the place where you live
but still appreciate coming home.

May God surround you with friends,
companions on the journey,
who will encourage and reassure you
and share love and laughter.

May you be secure in yourself,
growing in confidence and courage,
self-assured of your own worth and voice.

May you find joy in learning
and appreciate the privilege of time to consider the world and its ways.
May you be able to cope with the pressure of deadlines, essays and exams,
and through it all begin to discern your path in life.

May you explore radical dissent,
discover your own opinions through disagreement and argument,
debate and consensus
but never forget the value of the human person,
the wonder of creation
and that it is always worth listening.

And may you learn more of the God who fashioned and shapes us
and who challenges us to learn the ways of justice and peace.
For all your days and nights
may God the Father keep you in his gaze,
may God the Son keep you in his love,
may God the Spirit keep you near.
Amen

Simon Taylor

## Michael

Framed in the doorway
high on glue
Michael.

Between the outside cold
and the inside warmth
Michael.

Thirteen years of life
neither child nor man
Michael.

Michael – come in.

Ruth Burgess

## A search for wisdom (a prayer of confession)

God of wisdom,
when we have valued passive rote-learning
and the mechanical instilling of information
above genuine understanding and active exploration
FORGIVE US AND RENEW US IN OUR SEARCH FOR WISDOM.

God of truth,
when we have accepted glib solutions
and leapt to stereotyped conclusions
without a concern for accuracy and the careful weighing of evidence
FORGIVE US AND RENEW US IN OUR SEARCH FOR TRUTH.

God of justice,
when we have restricted education to a privileged elite
and discriminated against people
on grounds of race, gender, class or disability
FORGIVE US AND RENEW US IN OUR SEARCH FOR JUSTICE.

God of community,
when we have been possessive and competitive
with our knowledge and skills,
and envious and resentful of that of others
FORGIVE US AND RENEW US IN OUR SEARCH FOR COMMUNITY.

God of integrity,
when we have abused knowledge
to build up and sustain power over others,
and to exploit the earth's resources for our own ends
FORGIVE US AND RENEW US IN OUR SEARCH FOR INTEGRITY.

Jan Berry

## Blessing for students leaving home to study

For you, this is a new moment.
You have grown up among us,
you have been nurtured and shaped by communities of home and church,
communities others have chosen for you in love.

Now, it's your turn.
Go out and make choices.
Go and make friends.
Find those who think like you,
and those who think differently.

Look for places where you can grow,
where you can be challenged.

Look for new views.
Also look for places where you can find comfort,
where you can cry when you need to,
where you can pray.

Most of all, look for places where you can love.
You are our gift to the world.
We love you and send you into the world.
So love – actively, fiercely, humbly –
that the needs of the world might be soothed,
that Christ might walk with you in the places where you walk,
that the moment you are given might be met.

Katie Munnik

# A journey of learning

God of truth,
we praise you
for calling each one of us
to a unique journey of learning and discovery.
We thank you
for the joy of discovering new insights
and the exhilaration of struggling to grasp new understandings;
for the steady discipline which leads to a familiarity with a subject
and the readiness to use new skills;
for the ways in which the process of learning and teaching
shapes our interpretation of experience and our values.
WE PRAISE YOU AND CELEBRATE YOUR PRESENCE.

We thank you
for those who have studied before us
and whose research forms the foundation of our learning;
for those whose knowledge and skills are passed on
in spoken and written word,
in computer programmes and on the Internet;
for the companionship of those who share our struggles and frustrations,
and for the stimulus of debate and controversy.
WE PRAISE YOU AND CELEBRATE YOUR PRESENCE.

Jan Berry

## Coming of age

This day marks only
a passage of time,
yet somehow grants you maturity.
As you step out
into independence,
may you take with you:
the love of those who cared for you,
the guidance of those with wisdom to offer you,
the eagerness and enthusiasm of youth,
the lessons you have been taught
and those you have experienced for yourself,
and the willingness to learn
that life is unpredictable,
but that God can always be trusted …

whatever happens.

Marjorie Dobson

Celebrating friendship

## May God befriend us (opening responses)

In the excitement of new meeting,
MAY GOD BEFRIEND US WITH HOPE.

In the loyalty of companionship,
MAY GOD BEFRIEND US WITH TRUST.

In the grief of missing loved ones,
MAY GOD BEFRIEND US WITH COMFORT.

In the wonder of friendship,
MAY GOD BEFRIEND US WITH JOY.

Jan Berry

## Haikus for friendship

Walking together,
friends exploring the journey,
finding a new path.

Eating together,
friends breaking bread at a meal,
sharing news and hopes.

Growing together,
learning new ways of seeing,
reflecting on life.

Crying together,
supporting one another
through grief, hurt and pain.

Dreaming together,
longing for a new future,
working for justice.

Jan Berry

## The hidden gift

Holy Friend of all creation,
we praise you for the hidden gift of friendship,
often invisible or taken for granted,
overlooked in the social labels we use:
the daily bread of our living,
the salt that gives seasoning,
the water of our tears;
a treasure hidden in a field
but precious above rubies.

Jan Berry

## A celebration of friendship

For the friends who walk the way with us,
looking for signposts and helping us over obstacles,
marking the milestones on our journey:
WE GIVE THANKS TO THE GOD OF FRIENDSHIP.

For the friends we take for granted:
a steady presence to lean on,
a hand outstretched in our need:
WE GIVE THANKS TO THE GOD OF FRIENDSHIP.

For the friends who play with us,
lifting our spirits with humour and fun,
sparking off our imagination and dreams:
WE GIVE THANKS TO THE GOD OF FRIENDSHIP.

For the friends who work alongside us
in the companionship of shared tasks,
building our hopes and plans together:
WE GIVE THANKS TO THE GOD OF FRIENDSHIP.

For the friends who cry with us,
holding us when we are hurting
and embracing us with tender care:
WE GIVE THANKS TO THE GOD OF FRIENDSHIP.

For the friends who break bread with us,
sharing food and conversation,
putting the world to rights and laughing with us:
WE GIVE THANKS TO THE GOD OF FRIENDSHIP.

For the friends who dream with us,
praying and longing together for justice
and working for a vision of new humanity:
WE GIVE THANKS TO THE GOD OF FRIENDSHIP.

Jan Berry

## God, offer the hand of friendship (prayers of intercession)

To those who are cut off from friends
because they suffer illness or disability
which makes social interaction difficult,
or because unemployment has severed the daily routine
of working with colleagues:
GOD, COMPANION OF ALL,
OFFER THE HAND OF FRIENDSHIP.

To those who nurture friendship in unlikely places,
finding support and community
in hospital wards or prison blocks
or deprived areas where the shared struggle
helps community to survive:
GOD, COMPANION OF ALL,
OFFER THE HAND OF FRIENDSHIP.

To those who are separated from friends,
where distance has cut former ties,
where work or new relationships cause isolation;
for those moving to new areas,
needing to make connections and build networks:
GOD, COMPANION OF ALL,
OFFER THE HAND OF FRIENDSHIP.

To those making friendships in the midst of diversity,
crossing barriers of race or culture, class or age,
finding connections and common ground
that increase understanding and empathy,
and discovering differences that enrich their sharing:

GOD, COMPANION OF ALL,
OFFER THE HAND OF FRIENDSHIP.

To those whose friends have turned away,
forgetting to visit or failing to keep in touch
in the stress and pressure of daily life;
or rejecting them because of their way of life,
turning friendship to condemnation and betrayal:
GOD, COMPANION OF ALL,
OFFER THE HAND OF FRIENDSHIP.

For those in a church seeking to offer friendship,
looking beyond the familiar group and language
to welcome and befriend the stranger:
GOD, COMPANION OF ALL,
OFFER THE HAND OF FRIENDSHIP.

Jan Berry


## Thank you for my friends

For the friends I can depend on,
who are there when I'm in trouble:
Thank you for my friends.

For the friends who ask me questions,
who help me sort my life out:
Thank you for my friends.

For the friends I can relax with,
share a meal, a joke, a story:
Thank you for my friends.

For the friends I can cry with,
share my pain, my fears, my sadness:
Thank you for my friends.

For the friends who share my interests,
my concerns, my work for justice:
Thank you for my friends.

For the friends who think I'm crazy
but still love me and support me:
Thank you for my friends.

For the love that feels like friendship,
the love that keeps me going:
Thank you, God, my friend.

Ruth Burgess


## A closing blessing

May the blessing of God,
who plays alongside you in creation,
walks with you on your journey,
and inspires you with dreams for the future,
accompany you in love and friendship,
and welcome you home in joy.
Amen

Jan Berry

# Liturgies for celebrating relationships, marriages and partnerships

# Blessing for a civil partnership

**Gathering:**

*Folk gather in a circle.*

We stand together in this circle of family and friends who have shared A and B's journey over the past _____ years. They have entered into a civil partnership, which is recognised by law, and now they wish to seek God's blessing on their love and life together. But they are already blessed: they are blessed by the joy they find in each other; they are blessed by those who have kept faith with them in friendship and love. They are blessed because God is love and those who live in love live in God, and God lives in them. We love because God first loved us.

**Prayer of invocation:**

We gather in the name of God our creator,
who called us into life and made us for love.

We gather in commitment to Christ Jesus,
who calls us to follow and commanded us to love one another.

We gather in the presence of the Holy Spirit,
who calls us into community and strengthens us for living and for loving.

God of grace,
you have bound yourself to us in the covenant of the Word made flesh:
come among us,
that our celebration of life and love
may lead each of us further into fullness of life,
for the sake of Jesus Christ.
Amen

We're perhaps more used to vows being taken near the beginning of a relationship and not after a number of years. But perhaps it's appropriate for vows to be made when the dimensions – the shape and the character and the implications – of a relationship are known. So, to make vows is, for A and B, to say 'yes' to what has been, and to commit themselves to what is yet to be in their life together:

**The vows:**

*(The vows may be composed by the couple, or these, or similar vows, may be used.)*

Will you, A (or B), take B (or A)
to be your lifelong companion, lover and friend?

Will you spend your lives together, seeking to fulfil each other's needs,
growing together that you may share your strengths
and bear each other's weaknesses?

*A (or B):* I will.

Do you promise to love, honour and cherish *her/him*,
to dwell together in harmony and love as long as you both shall live?

*A (or B):* I do.

**Exchange of rings:**

As a symbol of these promises rings are now given and received: sign of the unbroken and unending love to which A and B are committed and of the trustworthy and eternal love of God.

*A (or B):* As a symbol of this covenant and our life together I give you this ring.

Friends, A and B have called us here to witness this act of commitment and to celebrate with them. We have shared their journey to this day. Please join with me as we commit ourselves to support and love them in the future:

**Congregational response:**

TOGETHER, AND IN THE SIGHT OF GOD,
WE WILL SUPPORT A AND B IN THEIR LIFE TOGETHER
AND IN THEIR LOVE FOR EACH OTHER.
WITH THEM, AND BY GOD'S GRACE,
WE WILL LIVE BY FAITH,
JOURNEY IN HOPE,
NURTURE AND SHARE LOVE WITH EACH OTHER
AND SERVE GOD'S WORLD.
FOR ALL THAT HAS BEEN,
WE ARE GRATEFUL.
FOR ALL THAT IS YET TO BE,
WE SAY 'YES'.
AMEN

In essence, God blessing us is God saying 'Yes to us'. So we ask God's blessing on A and B and on the vows that they have made. We shall embody this blessing by our action now:

*(The congregation is invited to encircle A and B and to lay hands on them as a sign of blessing.)*

The blessing:

*A and B say to each other:*

The Lord bless you and keep you.
The Lord be kind and gracious to you.
The Lord look upon you with favour
and give you peace.
Amen

We are blessed that we may be a blessing to each other and to the world. God says 'yes' to us that we might say 'yes' to God and to God's world. So I give each of you a charge:

Charge:

Let love be genuine; hate what is evil,
hold fast to what is good;
love one another with mutual affection;
outdo one another in showing honour …
Rejoice with those who rejoice,
weep with those who weep.

*(Romans 12:9–10,15)*

Prayers of celebration and concern:

Living, loving God, we believe that there is rejoicing in heaven
when two people fall in love and commit themselves to each other.
May our joy, laughter and prayers now reach up to heaven.

We pray for A and B,
giving thanks with them for all that has brought them to this day:
for those who gave them life and taught them how to love;
for those who have affirmed and challenged them over the years;
for those who are not here today yet whose love and memory lives on.

We pray for A and B,
that their love may overflow into the communities in which they live and work
and be a sign of your presence,
for this world needs sure signs of a loving, merciful God.

We pray for ourselves,
that we might each be strengthened by today
to live lives that are more receptive to the mysterious presence of each other,

in which the divine presence waits to be found.

O God, by your Spirit take our prayers
and those inward yearnings of our hearts
and weave them into that covenant which embraces us all;
for the sake of Jesus Christ, the Word made flesh.

**Benediction:**

On your hearts and on your homes,
the blessing of God.
On your tears and on your laughter,
the blessing of God.
On your lives and on your loves,
the blessing of the God of eternal life and love.
Amen

Blair Robertson

# Knitting lives together: a liturgy for the blessing of an interfaith partnership (Jewish and Christian traditions)

**Call to worship (from Psalm 146):**

Praise the Lord!
PRAISE THE LORD, O MY SOUL!
I WILL PRAISE THE LORD AS LONG AS I LIVE;
I WILL SING PRAISES TO MY GOD ALL MY LIFE LONG.

Happy are those whose help is the God of Jacob,
whose hope is in the Lord their God;
WHO MADE HEAVEN AND EARTH,
THE SEA, AND ALL THAT IS IN THEM.

Who keeps faith forever;
WHO EXECUTES JUSTICE FOR THE OPPRESSED.

The Lord watches over the strangers;
GOD UPHOLDS THE ORPHAN AND THE WIDOW,
BUT THE WAY OF THE WICKED,
GOD BRINGS TO RUIN.

The Lord will reign forever,
your God, O Zion, for all generations.
PRAISE THE LORD!

Opening prayer:

Blessed are you, Lord God,
Shaper of all that is,
who guards our goings out and comings in,
constantly renewing us and all the world.
Praise to your name.

God of quiet confidence,
who attends us even when we think we are far from you,
praise to your name.

God of steadfast strength,
who works great things through the least of us,
praise to your name.

When we bend the world and people around us out of shape,
have mercy on us.

When we despair of any help,
have mercy on us.

When distress and difficulty tear us into anxiety,
give us peace.

Blessed are you, Lord God,
Shaper of all that is,
who guards our goings out and comings in.
AMEN

Exchange of questions between the partners:

*A:*

Before God and these witnesses, we affirm our partnership.

*B:*

We do not make vows at this time, but rather commit ourselves to discovering a shared
language that we might use to describe our life together.

*A:*

Our life together will be a life of partnership. Will you help me understand what partnership means?

*B:*

By committing to a life of partnership, we are entering into a covenant. Will you help me understand what covenant means?

*A:*

By entering into a covenant, we are constructing a community. Will you help me understand what community means?

*B:*

By constructing a community, we are opening ourselves to others and committing ourselves to lives of hospitality. Will you help me understand what hospitality means?

*A:*

By committing ourselves to hospitality, we are dedicating ourselves to lives in pursuit of justice and compassion. Will you help me understand how justice and compassion intertwine?

*B:*

By dedicating ourselves to lives in pursuit of justice and compassion, we are pledging ourselves to a search for wisdom, lives of study and of wrestling with the ways of God. Will you help me learn the ways of God?

*A:*

By wrestling with the ways of God, we also attend to the world around us, while travelling as companions on our journey. Will you help me learn how to be a faithful companion?

*B:*

By travelling as companions in our journey, we seek to find a home together. Will you help me create that home?

*A:*

By creating a home, we knit our lives together for shelter, caring and intimacy, love and cherishing. Will you share these tasks, this adventure, with me?

*B:*

I will. Will you share these tasks, this adventure, with me?

*A:*

I will.

**Casting-on ceremony:**

*This liturgy used knitting as its central liturgical action. One partner cast on several stitches (the beginning of a blanket worked from the centre outwards), then guided the other partner in knitting several more, and then guests were invited to come and add their own stitches. The blanket was then finished by the couple at home. (If neither partner is proficient in knitting or crochet, another meaningful action may be substituted here.)*

*The knitting was preceded by the following blessing over the wool:*

Blessed are you, Lord God,
Shaper of all that is,
who fashions creation in your image and likeness,
and gives to us the gift of craft.
Blessed are you, Lord God,
Shaper of all that is.

**The affirmation of friends:**

*A and B:*

While our partnership creates a new family and a new home, we do not do this in isolation from the world. We are bound up with you and others in ties of friendship, held in the intricate fabric knit by many different communities.

As we build our lives together, we will constantly build and rebuild our relationships with each of you.

Thus we humbly ask:

Will you give us your blessing: pray for us and support us with the love and freedom that we need, as best you can?

*Friends:*

We will.

Prayer of blessings:

*Modelled on the 'Sheva Brachos' from the traditional Jewish marriage ceremony. To be recited over a cup of wine. Each blessing may be spoken by a different person.*

Blessed are you, Lord God, Shaper of all that is, Creator of the fruit of the vine.

Blessed are you, Lord God, Shaper of all that is: all creation mirrors your splendour and reflects your radiance.

Blessed are you, Lord God, Shaper of all that is, Creator of human beings. Bless this partnership that it be strong enough to support these two through whatever experience comes their way, as they come to know themselves and each other.

Blessed are you, Lord God, Shaper of all that is, who calls all people to be partners in the work of seeking justice and building peace.

Blessed are you, Lord God, Shaper of all that is, who glories in the intricate particularities of your creatures, giving each of us a chance to tell our own stories. Bless these two that they may delight in the wonder of the fact that they are so similar and so different.

Blessed are you, Lord God, Shaper of all that is, whose abundant blessings overflow, turning your people into blessings for one another and for all.

Blessed are you, Lord God, Shaper of all that is, who creates the blessings of joy and celebration, lover and beloved, glad song and jubilation, pleasure and delight, love and solidarity, friendship and peace. Soon may we hear – from the streets of *(the town, city)* to the hills of Jerusalem and beyond – the voice of joy, the voice of gladness, the voice of lover, the voice of beloved, and the voices of friends and guests from their feasts of song.

Closing blessings:

GRACIOUS GOD, LOOK UPON US IN YOUR LOVE
AND GRANT US YOUR BLESSING.
WE GIVE YOU THANKS FOR THE TREASURY OF EXPERIENCES
THAT HAVE ENRICHED OUR LIVES
AND FOR MANY MEMORIES.

FOR WORK TO DO AND TASKS ACCOMPLISHED,
FOR THE JOY AND SUFFERING
THAT HAS BEEN KNIT INTO THE FABRIC OF OUR YEARS,
WE PRAISE YOU.

*A and B:*

God of grace and mercy,
we offer you praise and thanks for our many friends here:
for people who have been kind to us and generous of their time,
for those who have taught us and listened to us,
for those who have accompanied us short distances
or a long time on our journey.
Keep them under the tender wings of your fierce love;
guide them through day and through night.
Bless them for their mercies, and make them blessings for others.
Guard them and protect them, and help them guard and protect each other.

GOD OF GRACE AND MERCY,
WE OFFER YOU PRAISE AND THANKS
FOR YOUR GIFT TO US OF *(names of partners).*

O GOD, WHOSE GLORY BINDS ALL THAT IS
BUT WHOSE PRESENCE CAN NEVER BE BOUND,
SUSTAIN ALL WHO ARE PARTNERS IN PILGRIMAGE,
AND ESPECIALLY *(names of partners).*
KEEP THEM UNDER THE FIERCE WINGS OF YOUR TENDER LOVE;
LEAD THEM AS THEY MAKE THEIR WAY,
AND SHELTER THEM WHEN THEY REST.
BLESS THEM FOR THEIR MERCIES,
AND MAKE THEM BLESSINGS FOR OTHERS.
GUARD THEM AND PROTECT THEM,
AND HELP THEM GUARD AND PROTECT EACH OTHER.

ENRICH OUR LIVES WITHIN YOUR COMMUNITIES OF COVENANT PEOPLES,
WHEREVER WE MAY BE.
THAT WE MAY CONTINUE TO WORSHIP AND SERVE YOU,
ALL THE DAYS OF OUR LIVES.

The Lord bless you and keep you.
The Lord's face shine upon you, and be gracious to you.
The Lord's eyes fix upon you, and give you peace.
AMEN

*Note: The prayers within the closing blessings have been inspired by the 'Moving and Journeying' section
of* The Book of Common Worship *of The Presbyterian Church in Canada (pp. 278–9).*

Mark Godin and Alana Vincent

# The blessing of a civil partnership in church

**Welcome and introduction:**

We are here to worship God and to celebrate the love which A and B have found in and for one another. The lead-up to this event has not always been easy, because sadly the special relationship that A and B have found with each other is not always appreciated or welcomed within society or, even more sadly, generally accepted within the church. So we are here not only to share in the joy of A and B and their families, to affirm our love and support for them, but also to express our admiration for their courage and to ask God's special blessing upon them.

**Hymn:** 'All are welcome' (CH4 198)

**Prayer:**

Loving God, as we lift up our voices to sing your praise, to affirm your generous love for all, so we open our hearts to give you thanks for all your goodness and for all the gifts of your love: your creative power that brought the world into being, your continuing presence in the midst of life, made human in Jesus Christ, with us still – guiding us, challenging and disturbing us, gracefully sustaining us. It is our joy, delight and comfort that we live our lives in your embrace, surrounded by the love that keeps no score of wrongs, bears all things, endures all things and hopes all things, the love that never gives up on us and never lets us go.

And we thank you today for the gift of human love, for the joy and fulfilment of deep relationships with one another, believing that love is your very presence: it's you we know and experience when we love and are loved, you we see reflected in everyone who loves us. It's you who blesses us when we find someone to love in complete openness and trust.

We thank you now for the love that A and B share, for the joy they have found in one another, for friendship deepening into love, and love deepening into certainty as they commit themselves to each other before you.

May they be assured of the support and prayers of all their friends who have gathered here today, and all others who wish them well; and may they be conscious also of your presence, giving them strength, hope and the promise of your continuing grace, through Jesus Christ our Lord. Amen

**The vows** *(said first by one partner, then the other):*

All that I am I give to you,
all that I have I offer to you,
and all that I am yet to be I promise to you.

In the presence of God and our family and friends I join my life with yours.
I will share in your dreams, I will trust you, help you,
listen to you, care for you and love you as no other than yourself.
In this I ask God's help now and in all the days to come.

**Symbolic action** *(the sharing of wine, salt and bread):*

*The wine*

*A:*

Let us drink from one cup to remember the glad times we shall share together.

*B:*

Blessed are you, eternal God, who creates the fruit of the vine.

*The salt*

*B:*

Let us taste this salt to remember the bitter and unhappy times we shall share together.

*A:*

Blessed are you, merciful God, who gives us strength for our suffering.

*The bread*

*A:*

Let us eat this bread to remember our daily bread and daily life together. May God hallow
the small and ordinary things of life through his blessing.

*B:*

Blessed are you, loving God, who brings forth bread from the earth.

**Song:** e.g. 'Brother, sister, let me serve you' (CH4 694), or 'For everyone born, a place at
the table' (CH4 685)

**Readings**

**Reflection**

**Prayer:**

God of compassion and justice, of generosity and grace, of loving faithfulness, you know us better than we know ourselves. You know that even when we mean well and have the best of intentions we do not always live up to what we say and want to do and be.

So as we rejoice in your blessing of A and B's loving commitment we pray that through the days ahead you may continue to surround them with your love, sustain them with your grace, inspire them with your hope, that they may be able to keep the vows they have made.

May they be loyal and faithful to one another throughout their life together, bearing each other's burdens and sharing each other's joys. May their home be a happy place, warm and welcoming to friend and stranger alike, filled with light and laughter and love. May they grow through each other's love and enjoy each other's life, and may their partnership be a blessing and an enrichment to all who know them.

Living God, at this time of happiness and celebration, help each one of us to live with compassion and integrity, to remember all those in need; and to give thanks for those dear ones who have influenced our lives for good and, having walked this way before us, are now safe with you forever.

We offer all these prayers in the name of Jesus Christ, who taught his friends to pray together *(Lord's Prayer)* …

**Song:** e.g. 'Glory to God above' (CH4 105)

**Benediction**

Norman Shanks

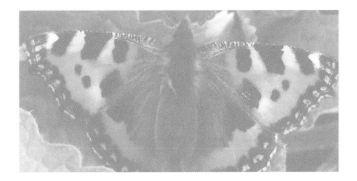

# A service of blessing

**Introduction:**

A and B have come here before you, their family and friends, to affirm and deepen their love and commitment to each other.

You are all part of this service, not an audience, and your love and prayers mean much to both of them.

We begin by coming together in a general prayer to God, or a higher power, and by opening ourselves up to the spirit inside each of us:

**Opening prayer:**

O Holy Spirit, who is known to us as Love,
we pray that in A and B's life
there may be concord and creativity
and love and laughter together.
Whatever the trials and testings
that may come before them,
may they find continuing faith and trust in each other;
and in their companionship, may they find peace.
As they continue to build their home together,
may it be bright with the conversation of many friends
and be a haven from tension.

*Folk are invited to reflect in silence on their wishes for A and B ...*

**Readings:** e.g. Poems ...

**Address:**

Relationships are wonderful, but they need tending from time to time, as any of us who are in or have been in long-term relationships will know. We want you both to go from strength to strength, secure in the love you feel. If you have times when you've got the 'ump' with each other, think about the vows you've made today. Think about the poems and readings that have just been recited. If you can do that, you won't go far wrong.

In a minute we, your family and friends, are going to stand with you and show our support for you in this new phase of your life together. As you make your vows, remember the love that surrounds you here in this place today.

**Declarations of hope:**

*Leader:*

We are gathered together today to celebrate the love which has brought A and B together. They would like you all to witness to their declarations of hope, followed by their vows of commitment.

Do you declare that you will recognise each other's freedom to grow as individuals, and allow each other the time and space to do so?

*A and B:*

We do declare this.

*Leader:*

Do you declare to bring strength and vision to your relationship, and courage and understanding?

*A and B:*

We do declare this.

*Leader:*

A, do you declare that you will give yourself wholly to B, sharing your love and your life, your wholeness and your brokenness, your joys and your sorrows, your riches and your poverty, your successes and your failures?

*A:*

I do declare this.

*Leader:*

B, do you declare that you will give yourself wholly to A, sharing your love and your life, your wholeness and your brokenness, your joys and your sorrows, your riches and your poverty, your successes and your failures?

*B:*

I do declare this.

*Leader:*

Guests, the ceremony in which we are now participating is a bold expression of love and joy. It gives public recognition to the love that A and B feel for each other, and the commitment they freely make to one another this day.

I therefore ask you to offer your support and love to A and B:

Do you, who know and care for A and B, give them your blessing now as they enter into this new stage of their relationship, and do you promise to give them your deepest love, understanding and support during both the good times and the bad?

*All:* We do.

**Blessing of rings:**

God of generosity and bounty,
bless these rings,
which we also bless in your name.

May A and B
see in these rings
a symbol of the love that never ends.

May they find gladness in each other,
in mutual giving and receiving.

May they be glad in the gift of their bodies,
in touch and passion,
in affection and goodwill.

May they bring to each other tact and generosity,
compassion and forgiveness.

May they share their joys and their sufferings,
their fears and their trust,
each giving the other room to grow
in freedom and in truth.

**Vows of commitment:**

A and B, I now invite you to join hands and make your vows, in the presence of God and surrounded by your family and friends.

*(Appropriate vows are made.)*

**Blessing and the proclamation:**

A and B, may the blessing of God Almighty,
the Father, the Son and the Holy Spirit,
be with you both
this day and for evermore.
Amen

Those whom God has joined together let no one put asunder.

In the presence of God and before this congregation, and earlier with the Registrar, A and B have given their consent and made their marriage vows to each other. They have declared their marriage by the joining of hands and by the giving and receiving of rings. I therefore proclaim that they are definitely husband and wife and truly blessed.

Kes Grant

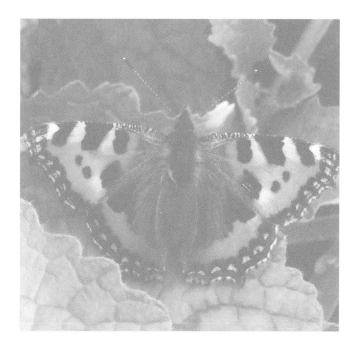

# Celebrating a relationship

**Words of gathering:**

A and B, you have done the honour of gathering us together to celebrate with you your love and to rejoice in your commitment to each other. We are so happy to be here and, believing that there is rejoicing in heaven whenever people love each other, we will ask for God's blessing upon your lives.

Today we remind ourselves that every human being finds true fulfilment in life by loving God and loving their neighbour. God has created us that we might grow in love.

From the earliest times women and men have made solemn vows before God and before witnesses. The stories of David and Jonathan and Ruth and Naomi remind us of two such vows, made before God, and calling upon God to bless the love they professed for each other.

**Prayer:**

God of love and creator of life,
we are here today so that A and B may speak of their love for each other
and that we may share in their happiness and joy.
We are thankful for all that has brought them to this stage in their life:
for the grace which has led them over obstacles,
the strength which has made them persevere
and the courage to accept themselves and each other as they are.

Gracious God, you are an exacting and faithful friend
who stands with us in life,
helping us to find joy and peace,
to create justice and freedom.
So may we all live as your friends
and as trusted companions to each other.
Amen

**Vows and the exchange of rings:**

Please respond to these questions by saying 'I do.'

Will you, A/B, take B/A to be your lifelong companion, lover and friend?

Will you spend your lives together, seeking to fulfil each other's needs, growing together that you may share your strengths and bear each other's weaknesses?

Do you promise to love, honour and cherish *her/him*, to dwell together in harmony and love as long as you both shall live?

*A/B:* I do.

You have chosen to exchange rings with each other …

**Prayer for the exchange of rings:**

O God, bless these rings:
grant that these who wear them
may always have a deep faith in each other.
May they do your will
and live together in peace and love,
sharing their joys and fears,
and each with patience,
giving the other room to grow in freedom and in truth,
through Jesus Christ our Lord.
Amen

*As the rings are exchanged, the couple say to each other:*

*A and B:* This ring is a sign of all that I am and all that I have.

Receive and treasure it as a token and pledge of the love that I have for you, and wear it as a protection whenever we are separated.

**A reading** *(perhaps by a friend)*

**Pledge of love and support:**

Finally, as you have pledged your love to and for each other, so we, as your friends, pledge to you our love and support, knowing that living in love is never easy and cannot be done in isolation, but requires people around who are loyal and generous. We want to be those people for you, and may God help us to be so.

**Blessing:**

On your hearts and on your homes, the blessing of God.
On your loving and on your laughter, the blessing of God.
On your hopes and on your fears, the blessing of God.
On your lives, the blessing of the God of life eternal.
Amen

Blair Robertson

# A wedding service/blessing of a partnership

Hymn

Introduction:

Dear A and B, we are gathered here today to celebrate your love for each other. Having found one another, and grown in understanding and love together, you now want to seek the blessing of God and the support of your friends and relatives in a public act of commitment.

This service does not have magical properties. It will not create a relationship that does not already exist. It is a time to put down a marker, to say: '*From this day on we will go forward together, sharing all that we can, supporting each other in difficulty and loving each other in all times and in all ways.*'

It is a time for making vows and declaring intentions, and for facing the uncertainties of the future with the one thing of which you are certain: your love for one another and the hope that your love will last forever.

Opening prayer:

Lord, our God, you have given us this day:
a day of expectation and of joy;
a day of solemnity and of happiness;
a day of certainty and of hope.
This day is a day of new beginnings.
So, loving God, we ask that you will hear our prayers,
know our thoughts
and enable A and B to grow in grace and love
all the days of their lives.
Amen

Readings

Statement of intentions:

*Leader:*

A and B, the Bible says that love is patient and kind, that it is not envious or rude. It does not insist on its own way; it is not irritable or resentful; it does not rejoice in wrongdoing, but rejoices in the truth. It bears all things, believes all things, hopes all things, endures all things. This love never ends.

Such love might seem almost unattainable, yet it is the love for which you hope.

In this light will you, A, do all that you can to show love to B?

*A:*

I will.

*Leader:*

In this light will you, B, do all that you can to show love to A?

*B:*

I will.

*Leader:*

I ask you both:

Will you seek to learn from one another; to be patient in understanding and loving in action?

Will you seek to forgive each other's failings and to build each other up in love?

Will you seek to be faithful to each other today, tomorrow and forever?

*A and B:*

We will.

**Exchange of vows:**

*Leader:*

You have publicly stated your intentions, and now I ask you to seal those intentions with your vows.

A, take B's hand in yours, saying after me:

*A:*

I love you and, as far as it is in my power, I will always love you.
I give you all I have and all I am.
I trust you and honour you.
When times are difficult I will stay beside you.
To this end I give you my life to keep.

*Leader:*

B, take A's hand in yours, saying after me:

*B:*

I love you and, as far as it is in my power, I will always love you.
I give you all I have and all I am.
I trust you and honour you.
When times are difficult I will stay beside you.
To this end I give you my life to keep.

**Exchange of rings:**

*As the couple exchange rings these words are said:*

For centuries rings have been a symbol of commitment. The circle of the ring never ends.
And so as these rings are exchanged, we pray together:

MAY THE LOVE THAT A AND B HAVE FOR EACH OTHER
BE NEVER-ENDING.

**Hymn**

**Final prayer:**

God bless A and B as they continue on the journey of life together.
May their love for each other be renewed from day to day.
May their capacity to care be refreshed from day to day.
May they always turn to each other for support and love,
confident of meeting each other's needs.

Together let us pray for *A* and *B*:

MAY THEY BE FRIENDS,
MAY THEY BE LOVERS.
MAY THEY KNOW CARE,
MAY THEY KNOW COMFORT.
MAY THEIR LOVE GROW STRONGER DAY BY DAY,
AND MAY THEY ALWAYS KNOW FULFILMENT IN EACH OTHER'S COMPANY.

CARING GOD, POUR YOUR LOVE AND JOY INTO THEIR LIVES,
THAT THEIR LOVE AND JOY MAY BE COMPLETE.
IN JESUS' NAME. AMEN

Andrew Pratt

Sentences and blessings for marriage
and partnership ceremonies

May your constant love be with us, God,
as we put our hope in you.

Psalm 33:22

Love is patient and kind; it is not jealous or conceited or proud.
Love is not ill-mannered or selfish or irritable.
Love does not keep a record of wrongs.
Love never gives up;
and its faith, hope and patience never fail.

1 Corinthians 13:4–6 (Good News Bible)

Bless to me, O God, the sky that is above me.
Bless to me, O God, the earth that is beneath me.
Bless to me, O God, your beauty all around me.
Bless to me, O God, the bed companion of my love.

Carmina Gadelica (adapted)

Love is as strong as death.
It burns like fire, like a mighty flame.
Many waters cannot quench love;
mighty rivers cannot wash it away.

Song of Solomon 8:6,7

God to enfold you.
God to surround you.
God in your speaking.
God in your hoping.

God in your lives.
God in your hearts.
God in your loving.
God in your belonging.

Carmina Gadelica (adapted)

Blessed are those, O God, who enter your house,
those who praise you.
Blessed are those whose strength is in you,
those who walk in your ways.

Psalm 84:4–5

The company of God be yours
the company of the God of life.

The company of Christ be yours,
the company of the Christ of love.

The company of the Holy Spirit be yours,
the Holy Spirit of grace.

The company of the Three be yours
today, tomorrow and all your lives.

Carmina Gadelica (adapted)

God will be your keeper.
God will defend you.
God will be with you when you come in.
God will be with you when you go out.
God who made the heavens and the earth.
God will be your help.

Taken from Psalm 121:2–8

Peace between friends,
Peace between family,
Peace between lovers,
in love of the God of life.

Carmina Gadelica (adapted)

Nothing,
nothing we can imagine,
nothing that exists,
can ever separate us
from the love of God.

Romans 8:38,39

The sacred Three
to bless
to shield
to surround your hearth
your home
your household

this night and day
this day and night
and every day and night.

Carmina Gadelica (adapted)

Today
may you be held in each other's love,
may you be blessed by your family and friends,
may you sing and dance for joy.

Ruth Burgess

Spring
summer
autumn
winter
day after night after day.

Live well your lives
with courage and justice.
Share your love.
Be cherished.
Be blessed.

Spring
summer
autumn
winter
day after night after day.

Ruth Burgess

The blessing of the sun and moon be yours
and a million twinkling stars.

The blessing of the hills and seas be yours
and a chorus of birds and whales.

The blessing of laughter and tears be yours
and a hug of warmth and strength.

The blessing of many days be yours,
a journey blessing of love.

Ruth Burgess

Bits and pieces for celebrating relationships, marriages and partnerships

## A family wedding blessing

May your home be a place
of love and joy and justice.

May your children come in and out
in warmth and contentment.

May friends and strangers
find a welcome within your walls.

A blessing on your wedding
a blessing on your life together
a blessing on your children.

A blessing on this day
and all the days that stretch before you.

A blessing of the Maker
a blessing of the Storyteller
a blessing of the Breath of life.

Ruth Burgess

## An opening statement for a partnership ceremony or wedding

Let us worship God:

God makes people in God's own image;
God who, in the beginning, said:
'It is not good to be alone.'

God is love,
and those who live in love,
live in God
and God lives in them.

David Coleman and Zam Walker

# Three wedding/civil partnership memories and ideas

During weddings and civil partnerships I always turn the couple round so they are facing the congregation, and I stand slightly off to one side. Why should everyone come and look at me and see the backs of the people they know and love?

Kes Grant

I was at a former colleague's wedding recently, and they passed the rings round the congregation before the vows so that each person could hold them and say a prayer or make a wish. I thought that was lovely.

Catherine Harkin

I remember one of the first weddings I conducted, in Gorbals in the 1960s. It was between a drummer of a heavy rock band and a teacher. They wanted it to take place at 2:00am in the Citizens' Theatre, and they wanted me to turn up in full clericals, and do the whole thing by the book! So I did – and when it came to sharing the Lord's Prayer, sitting there surrounded by the sweaty bodies of young people, most of whom had probably not been at a service of worship for a very long time, I still remember the quietness as we spoke the words together …

John Harvey

# Including the guests

At our preparation discussion the bride was distressed. Not only had her grandfather died recently, several older relatives could not make the long journey from the USA. She really wanted them included, but could not see how to do it. After talking through her grief, I suggested we light candles at the beginning of the service to represent those living and deceased who were missing from the wedding. The idea met with approval from the bride and groom.

We used a small table placed to one side of where the couple would stand at the sanctuary steps. On it were the candles, one for each missing relative. As the bride reached the chancel steps, I lit a taper from the Easter candle, which we always light for weddings, and lit the representative candles from it. The reasons for doing this were explained in the general welcome to everyone.

Chris Polhill

## A wedding prayer

Melody and words: Carol Dixon
Arrangement: Isabel Morrison

♩ = 88

God, pour your bless-ing now on this cou-ple stand-ing be-fore you, bound by their love,

pledg-ing to keep and trea-sure each oth - er, made one in you through Je-sus your son.

May all their days be bright with your ra-di-ance, as on this day with joy they are filled;

give them your strength when trou-bles dis-heart-en them, mould-ing their lives to fol-low your will.

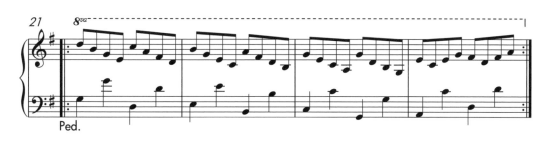

God, pour your bless-ing now on this cou - ple join-ing their lives to - geth-er this day;

grant them your peace be - yond un-der- stand -ing, blest by your grace each step of the way.

poco rit.

## The perfect couple

She likes cars
and I like walking.
She likes films
and I like dancing.
But together
I put a spring in her step
and she sets my engine racing.

She has a dog
and two cats own me.
She likes the city
and I like the country.
But together
we stroke and stretch and curl up
and every place is home.

She works for the Revenue
and I work for the Church.
She writes thrillers
and I write prayers.
But together
our minds click, our words spark
and our spirits soar to the heavens.

Jan Berry

## This is your day

This is your day.
The day when love, for you,
has turned full circle.
You were conceived in love,
cherished at birth,
nurtured through childhood,
carefully supported
as you learned to face the world
in the challenging arena
of adulthood.

Now, you step out together,
secure in the trust you have found,
to begin a new life of love –
and the circle turns.
Responsibility for loving
becomes your own,
and the vows you share
seal your promises
to enfold this new relationship
with a deepening love.

We, who have loved you
for so long,
bless you in your loving.

Go with God,
for God is the source of our being,
the centre of your circle,
the focus of all love.

Marjorie Dobson

## Blessings and vows

*Vows of the partners:*

In the presence of these witnesses, I take you as my constant friend, my faithful partner and my love.

I promise to go on giving you the best of myself.

I promise to continue to respect you as your own person and to realise that your interests, needs and desires are no less important than my own.

I promise to continue sharing with you my time and attention and to bring joy and laughter and strength and imagination to our relationship.

I promise to keep myself open to you, to let you see through the window of my world into my innermost thoughts and feelings and dreams.

I promise to keep growing along with you, to be willing to face changes in order to keep our relationship alive and exciting.

I promise to continue loving you in good times and in bad, with all I have to give and all I feel inside, and to nourish our love so that it deepens between us for as long as we live.

*A candlelit blessing from the parents:*

We light these candles to honour the loving relationships handed down through the generations, of those present and not present, and to welcome the coming together of two families in the union of A and B.

May the light of love burn brightly in your lives and bless you down all the years to come, as you create a union of your own.

*A candlelit blessing from the grandparents:*

A and B, as we love your parents, so we love you. We pledge to love you and to share our wisdom and strength in the service of you.

May the light of these candles be a symbol of the light of love in your life together.

*A blessing for the couple from friends and guests:*

Divine spirit of love, we are thankful for the gift of A and B in our lives.

We ask that your healing spirit illuminate their minds with your wisdom, enrich their hearts with your love and feed their souls with your peace.

Give them the courage to truly embody the vows of commitment that they have made here today, and may their cherished promises to one another inspire us all in committing to being the kindest, most loving and generous people we can be.

Fill us with your grace to support A and B in bringing out the best in one another, now and forever.

Stephen Wright

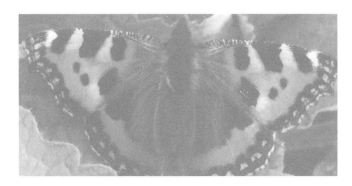

# Love poems for a wedding (to Lindy and Bill)

**Love at a wedding**

You rarely see love at a wedding.
It is no bad thing – her habits are unsuitable.

Love does not dress up –
she is as happy in a sack as a silk dress.

Love does not care for ritual,
and she has complex relations with the clergy.

Love does not gossip.
She already knows where she stands with everyone.

Love is not malleable.
She has a will like gravity.

Love creates chaos everywhere she goes –
breaks hearts, provokes crazy behaviour.

Love bursts out singing, without asking,
tunes hardly anybody knows.

Why, then, would anyone invite love to a wedding?
And yet, I think I saw her earlier:

Coming between old married couples, as she does;
perhaps even between the bride and groom.

Shame on her – doesn't she know better?
Show her the door, and let normality resume.

Brave words – nevertheless, you know:
Once love is in, she may not choose to go.

**No poem about love**

There is no poem about love that tells the truth.
How could it? Love is too varied,
shifting its shape like Proteus in the myth;
too sharp-edged, too airy,
too dark, too dazzling,
too obvious – too amazing.

The multiplicity of love is like the forces
that bind everything:
gravity holding planets on their courses,
magnetic fields, and the tight strings
that rein a nucleus
within its tiny space.

I say: as forces bind the universe
love binds humanity.
We can be bound by choice,
but the will wearies
and is gone:
while love binds on.

Interplays of the forces create lightning
and the stability of rock;
the roar of water tumbling,
and the deep pool it strikes;
the snowflake's intricacy
and the wind's simplicity.

Love constantly changes too;
from the unsteady dance
that it first puts us through,
to iron confidence.
Passion transforms
and becomes utter calm.

And a kaleidoscope of bonds
in dazzling colours
links daughters and sons,
sisters and lovers;
and binds our own
splintered selves into one.

I say: never ask love
to be one thing;
set your love free to move,
constantly changing.
Trust the reality,
and not what poets say.

**Love come again**

'Love is come again', you sang
at another wedding in a sweet voice,
'again like wheat that springeth green.'
Such slow, soft images.

From what I saw,
love came again more like wild injuns
appearing on the skyline round the wagon train –
whooping down carrying emergency supplies of whisky
and big ornamental pipes.

More like Evel Knievel
busting the screen
on a red Harley Davidson,
flying through flaming hoops,
roaring like fifteen tigers
in a pen.

Love come again
with teeth and tails
and flashing eyes.
And by the time your heads clear,
why, the wheat is ten feet tall
and every grain is melon-sized.

Roddy Cowie

# Love has brought you here

Love has brought you here today.

Love can hold you together
when even the most patient person would say:
'Enough is enough.'

Love can keep you listening to each other
when even the most rational person would say:
'I've heard all I need to hear.'

Love can find a way to knit you together:
when you've felt unforgiven,
when you've been unkind,
when you question the value of a vow.

Three things: faith, hope and love –
three mysterious things that remain when all else blows away.
Those things come from God, and they are good.
They can be depended on.

Today brings great honour to your families who lovingly nurtured you,
and to the future you will forge together.

Love has brought you here today –
and we here with you are so thankful that we are your witnesses.

*(Names of partners)*, we are here to worship God,
the creator of love,
and we are here to celebrate with you
because your new life together embodies and reflects
God's joyful purpose.

The blessings of Christ be with you
as you walk into your new life together.

Sally Foster-Fulton

## You came here to make it sacred

You didn't just come here today to make it official: you came here today to make it *sacred*.

Sacred means *'set apart, distinct, worthy of a framework and boundaries, holy'*. And by coming here today and standing together in front of your friends, you have said that this relationship is sacred to the two of you and that you will cherish and protect it.

And we gather here with you as witnesses, and silently promise to help you – to uphold you – because sacred is not always simple.

You didn't just come here today to make it official: you came here today to make it *sacred*.

God bless you both, today and always.

Sally Foster-Fulton


## How I became a fundamentalist

Morning, God – how are things today?

*Well, it's a beautiful day, but my people are messing it up already. I didn't give them fire so they could make bombs, did I? I gave them food to share. I gave them gifts of healing and caring that they were supposed to share, too. I gave them a beautiful garden, and now they're trashing it. I made them all shapes and colours to make them interesting for each other, but they don't like it. Why aren't you doing something about it?*

What, me, God?

*Yes, you.*

But I don't know where to start!

*I gave you the book on it! Haven't you read it?*

That's a trick question! Of course I've read it.

*What's so difficult about it then?*

Ask Job – he'll tell you!

*I'm asking you …*

Well, God, I keep stalling, right there at the beginning where it says that you took a look at what you'd made, and you liked it.

*And so I did. What's wrong with that? I still like it. I wish you did, too.*

Eh? I do. It's all fine with me, except … Well, you know, what about the Fall, then? Didn't that change anything?

*No. What was good then is good now. The Fall is what you lot are doing with my gifts to you. You don't have to bomb your brothers and sisters to liberate them from your other brothers and sisters. They don't have to starve while you get fat. And if you want to get personal, just yesterday you complained about the weather. You said it was too hot. A couple of days earlier you complained that it was too wet. Then you complained that one of your customers was a wooden-brained dolt. Whose creation do you suppose he is, eh?*

All right, Lord. I didn't really mean it.

*Too late. You should hear what he was saying about you.*

Much rather not, thanks all the same. I think I can guess. But that's not what I wanted to talk to you about this morning.

*I wondered when you were going to get to the point.*

Well, God, it's about our younger daughter.

*Yes. A lovely child.*

You know, I always thought your people were meant to pair off, one of each, raise families and just do, you know, ordinary things.

*Go on.*

It isn't happening.

*You're sure about that?*

She and her girlfriend are getting married.

*I know, and I am as happy as her parents must be to see her so happy, getting ready to make her life with the person she loves best in the world. Those two will make the world a better place. It's good.*

Was that part of what they meant when they said you saw it all, and it was good?

*Of course it was.*

I don't get it. It wasn't part of what they wrote before that bit – you know, Adam and Eve and all that?

*What? You expected the whole of my creation to be revealed in the first chapter? I like molecules and atoms too. I was very fond of the dinosaurs, and I created Kirk sessions to make sure we didn't forget them. I like punk rockers and their music. I like your autistic friend's poetry. But nobody knew about any of those things back then. I like all kinds of people and things that have taken the rest of my people thousands of years to discover and understand and enjoy. In fact, I love them.*

I'll tell our daughter you said that.

*Good. I knew you would.*

Andrew Foster

## Blessing of a marriage (at a family gathering)

A and B, in seeking God's blessing on your marriage and God's grace in your continuing journey together and in the life of your family, do you reaffirm the vows that you took when you were married: promising to be a faithful husband and wife to one another, to love, comfort, protect and honour each other as long as you both shall live?

*(A and B say 'We do.')*

May God bless you and guard you,
may God's face shine upon you,
may God be gracious to you,
look kindly on you and give you peace,
today and always.
Amen

Loving God, may your ever-dependable love surround A and B, indeed surround us all; may your amazing irresistible grace enable them to continue to keep the promises they made to one another on their wedding day. Fill them with your joy and guide them in your way this day and always. Continue to bless their home and family life. Help us all to be faithful to the light and values by which we seek to walk.

And the blessing of God,
Creator, Son and Holy Spirit,
be upon us all now and evermore.
Amen

Norman Shanks

## Do you realise what you've just said?

Do you realise what you've just said? 'I give myself to you' – that's big stuff. From now on, this person standing beside you is you. And every decision you make from now on – every wish, every hope, every desire – is not just yours. God knows, the only way that this can work is if both of you want what is best for the other one – first and foremost – deep down at your core. That kind of mutual adoration will take you far. It will take you to a new place entirely, open doors to feelings you've never had … because when you want everything for somebody else, and they want that for you, you are adding love to faith and hope, and when you walk the road looking out for each other, it's easier to find middle ground.

Do you realise what you've just said? 'I give myself to you' – that's big stuff: I give you all the things deep down that make me *me* … I hand over my dreams, my big ideas and little hopes. I place them into your hands for safekeeping. I trust you with all the fears and insecurities nobody else knows about because I have tried so hard to keep them hidden, but no longer … I will share them with you. I will entrust you with my very soul, because we have promised today to protect each other and guard those secret, sacred places. I have discovered that you are able to take even those difficult parts of me, graft them gently into the whole of me, and see beauty … not that you don't see the flaws, but you have embraced them as part of loving me.

Do you realise what you've just said? 'I give myself to you' – that's big stuff. Because you are taking a stand today: Here is my solid foundation – I will go out from this place for the rest of my life. God has given us each other – to have and to hold from this day forward.

*(Names of partners)*, you are for each other solid ground: 'Where you go, I go.' This is what you said when you said 'I give myself to you.' That's big stuff.

Thanks be to God.

Sally Foster-Fulton

## No one is given away

Like many young women, when I got married, I disliked the idea of being 'given away': since I am not a possession to be traded. However, my dad very much cherished the idea of walking his daughter down the aisle and being involved in that moment, as I did.

Stewart and I wrote our own wedding service, and this is what we came up with for the part of the service where traditionally the bride is 'given away'. It could be easily adapted:

*The bride and groom and their parents stand.*

*Elizabeth and Stewart:* In this service no one is given away. As equal partners, we each remain our own person, and this strengthens our relationship. Our families do not give away their relationship with us, but continue to offer the love and support that has brought us to adulthood and to this day.

*Elizabeth's parents:* We welcome Stewart into our family and offer our love and support to you both.

*Stewart's parents:* We welcome Elizabeth into our family and offer our love and support to you both.

*The parents sit down.*

Liz Delafield


# Love is the circle

*(Tune: Slane)*

Love is the circle that holds and enfolds,
as journeying onwards the future unfolds.
May God be our guard, our companion and friend,
may grace keep us faithful, may hope have no end.

God, give us patience to listen and learn,
to value the gifts that we never could earn.
When living is challenged and tensions are rife,
may love help us cope with the stresses of life.

God, deepen friendship and help us to find,
as one with each other, new ways to be kind;
then bind us together, bring new love to birth,
as long as we live as companions on earth.

On from this moment we go in God's grace;
we walk hand in hand filled with joy from this place;
we know in God's Spirit our lives are now bound,
in love we find heaven – let heaven resound!

Andrew Pratt

## We meet at one point (a blessing)

We meet at one point,
at this intersection of our days,
one moment of your lives.

And here and now,
within this place,
the image of your love
stands clear before us.

Welcomed, we witness,
sharing your joy,
sending you forward
with love and support.

May your love grow and deepen.
May you look back to this time,
this moment,
and say that it was good.

Go, then, to the rest of your life,
and go in love.

Andrew Pratt

## Life comes to us strangely

Life comes to us strangely, Lord God. We don't ask for it, we just become conscious some-time after birth that we are living and have to make something of our lives. We don't choose our parents, nor do they choose us. We just have to learn to make the best of life with one another. We don't choose our bodies or our gender. We just have to learn to make positive use of what we are given. We don't choose when, where, how we will die. We just know that there will come a day when we hand over life and leave the earth.

So it matters to us what the psalmist says: that you, our God, have known us since we were a tiny speck in the womb, have loved us and cherished us through our life, and will receive us when it ends. That gives life meaning.

Love also comes to us strangely, Lord God. We do not dream it up and wish it on another, nor are we victims in turn. It seems to come from beyond, setting its claim upon two people – claiming them for each other and for a loving life in the world. There is something mysterious in the magnetic attraction people discover for one another, something they did not plan but which they could receive with joy. It's the Lord's doing and marvellous in our eyes. Not a matter for self-congratulation but for thanksgiving.

We bless you this day, Lord God, that A and B were captured together in the embrace of love; that they want to share their lives, with all the ups and downs that will entail: that they say so this day before you and in public, taking vows of faithfulness which yield joy and peace whatever circumstances have to be faced, because the foundation is love.

As you, Lord God, loved us, teach us to love one another, selflessly and enduringly. In your name we ask it. Amen

Ian M. Fraser

## On their way

We send A and B on their way,
praying that they may have lifelong delight in one another
and that their life together
will enrich all relationships of those who cross their path.

Let their shared life be a new glory which you add to the world.
We ask it in Jesus Christ's name.
Amen

Ian M. Fraser

## Prayer for a wedding anniversary

Celebrating God,
whose love enfolds the whole of life,
who calls us into union with you and with one another,
and who in creation blessed the partnership of marriage:
on this wedding anniversary day,
grant to your servants A and B,
and to all who celebrate with them,
thankful hearts for all that is past,
joyful hearts for this day's blessings
and hopeful hearts for what is still to come.
In the name of God the Maker, Son and Spirit,
one God in community.
Amen

Terry Garley

## She who shares life with me

I give thanks for the partner who shares life with me,
who sees something in me which escapes others,
who knows my faults and still loves me,
who appreciates my strengths and gives me confidence.
I give thanks for the partner
through whom I get glimpses into your nature, Lord God.
For you, too, know me through and through and still love me;
you forgive me generously and stay at my side.
It was your pleasure to bring us together.

Bless the Lord, O my soul:
let all that is within me bless God's holy name.
Amen

Ian M. Fraser

## Dreams take flesh

You open me
to tenderness and vulnerability,
my body aching with need of yours,
breathless and wobbly with wanting you.

You delight me
with your earthy laughter,
the tales that meander into mirth,
the sparking of fun and wit.

You seduce me
into a passion that holds you precious,
that grasps and cradles you,
fierce in my tenderness,
loving in my wildness.

You hold me
with the everyday comfort
of shared meals and TV,
snatched texts and long conversations,
the growing routine of togetherness.

You stretch out to me
the unexpected gift of love
and the promise of a future
where dreams take flesh,
lived in our bodies;
and hope makes its dwelling
in our home.

Jan Berry


## A prayer for understanding

God of all humanity,
you created each and every one of us
in your own image.
Enable us to accept those whose views
and ways of living and of loving
may differ from our own.
Make us willing to celebrate our differences
as part of your unending gift of variety.

Help us to learn
from each other's experience of your grace,
and above all,
let our bond to one another
be through our faith in Christ,
which goes beyond human distinctions.

May we all, as your people,
witness to your love in our lives.
Amen

James Curry

## Love grows

Love grows
love laughs
love sings
love cares
love cries
love dances
love does

Love is beautiful
love is powerful
love is exciting
love is hopeful
love is warm
love is a journey
love is

love takes risks
love makes you vulnerable
love asks questions
love tells stories
love stands up for justice
love gets you
love does

So be warned you lovers
you learners
you adventurers
be warned
though you can never be ready
love beckons
love grows
love changes lives
love does

Ruth Burgess

# Breakdown of relationships

## Divorce

Before God
we promised forever,
but it lasted three years.

The hopes and the blessings combined
were not enough
to quell the rising tide of aggravation
with which we seemed to annoy each other
that grew until
inevitably
we agreed to part.

God, were you there in those blessings so keenly meant?
Were you joking when the vows were pronounced unbreakable?

We didn't break them,
we just found it impossible
to fulfil them.

So forgive us.
Help us to learn to know ourselves,
to avoid unrealistic expectations.
Help us to recognise true love
based on honesty when
occasionally
it appears.

John Butterfield

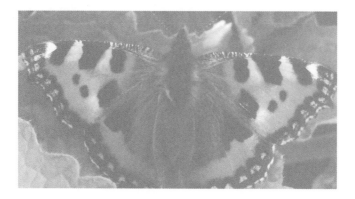

## Prayer for spouses who are separated

God of the sparrow, the stars, the waters, the light and reconciliation,
as we crawl under the covers,
having survived another day,
we tell the moon goodnight
and give you thanks for:

porches with rocking chairs and swings,
naming the colours of the sunset with children,
boats and jumping off docks,
wine and laughter,
friends who bring chocolate cake for breakfast,
friends who radiate hope,
friends who offer their guest rooms,
friends who make sure we eat a real meal,
friends who are devastated because they love us both,
the families we were born into
and the families we've chosen,
the cleansing salt of tears,
the unconditional love of pets,
texts and e-mails to read again and again
when the darkness is too much,
the ability to continue to breathe in and out,
the energy to be angry and yell,
the gift of allowing others to help,
the grace to forgive and be forgiven,
the dawning of another day,
and the promise of the Light
that no darkness can ever really overcome …

Our only response is gratitude.
In the name of the One
who is our greatest hope and comfort in this life.
Amen

Ashley-Anne Masters

## War hangs heavy between us

The violent emotions of anger from betrayal
have flown in the thunderclouds of despair,
but war still hangs heavy between us,
dark, desolate and wounding.
For the moment, the peace talks are futile,
there is no common ground,
for cruel words have bled our hearts dry
and tainted our memories of precious moments.

No longer will we share the knowing look
across a crowded room,
with the hint of embraces to come,
the touch of skin on skin –
breath on breath,
complacent in our togetherness.

The war is over.
There is an end to the fighting.
But the devastation of shattered lives is left behind
lingering in the dust of brokenness.
There is no victory.
You have gone – I will stay.
I will seek to heal wounds in the comfort of Christ
through the minefield and craters of abandonment
until there is a peace between us.

Looking forward I cannot find you.
The scarred battlegrounds of divorce
have changed the horizons.
All I can do to move onwards is to trust in God.
Trust that we will reach that place of peace.

Christine Green

## It does not take much (a poem at breaking point)

It does not take much
to sink a ship
that is already foundering.

What a galleon in full sail
on a broad calm ocean
would have embraced
and contained
with some ease,
can be too much for a ship
already in difficulties.

A broken promise,
an angry telephone call,
a confidence betrayed,
an unanswered e-mail
and a changed timetable.

These have caused me
to jump ship
and leap
into dark
uncharted
waters.
Better the devil
you don't know.

June Boyce-Tillman

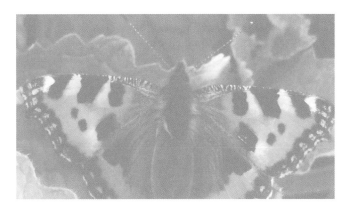

## My petition for divorce

God, the Father,
who took the risk of making us male and female
and called us in partnership to replenish and care for the earth,
look kindly, I pray, on my petition for divorce.

God, the Son,
who condemned the one-sided, unfair divorce practice of your day,
which gave one partner the power to get rid of the other without just cause,
look with understanding on my cause, which I believe to be just.

God, the Holy Spirit,
who led Saint Paul to see that we are all one in Christ Jesus,
open the eyes of others to my plight,
and to the calling to be no longer slaves
but to enjoy the freedom Christ won for us.

I do not say that I am without blame;
but I do say that, made as I am in your image,
I was meant to have a life which expresses that reality –
not one constantly devalued, at the mercy of another's whims and moods,
given no space and respect to mature and flourish in my own right
as heir to your promises.

Grant me the grace,
should divorce proceedings produce fundamental change,
to review our situation afresh;
and if it does not,
to realise that it might be right for both that two people
should be saved any longer from living a lie.
Amen

Ian M. Fraser

# After the Decree Absolute

*It is assumed that there will have been pastoral counsel before this service.*

*Family members and friends may be present at the wish of the pilgrim. If both ex-partners are present the liturgy could be adapted.*

*Minister:*

The peace of God be with you.

*Pilgrim:*

And also with you.

*Pilgrim kneels.*

*Minister:*

Living God, who walks beside us in both trouble and joy, we come to offer to you the sorrow and pain of the failure of the marriage of *(name)* and *(name)*. We thank you for the love they first knew and shared *(and for their child/ren, _____)*. You, who know the secret thoughts of all our hearts, understand the struggle and difficulty of the past *months/years*, and we come for your loving forgiveness and healing, now that this marriage has ended. Bless this time of prayer, that through it *(name)* may know your blessing and direction for *her/his* life now. Amen

*Pilgrim:*

I confess before God that I am unable to keep the marriage vows I made with *(name)*. I am sorry that *(here specific causes for the marriage breakdown may be named, if wished)* this means the promises I made cannot be kept, and I ask for your forgiveness and healing. Amen

*Minister:*

Almighty God, who knows the secrets of your heart, forgives you for the failure of your marriage, and is beside you as you live with the continuing consequences.

*Pilgrim:*

I return my wedding ring to the church.

*The minister accepts the wedding ring on a prayer book, and places the book and ring on the altar.*

*Minister:*

I accept this ring in the name of the church. It is returned to God, and before God your marriage is ended. *(The ring can later be sold and the money given to charity.)*

*Silence*

**Prayers** *(adapt as necessary):*

Bless *(name)* and *(name)* in their separate lives. May they come to forgive each other and find new life. Bless them in the care of their children, and in all the places where they will meet and need to cooperate. God in your mercy …

*Pilgrim and all present:* Hear our prayer.

*Minister:*

Living God, we pray for your blessing on all those affected by this divorce.

Bless the children *(names)*. May they know that each parent truly loves them, and know your presence with them in their new way of living. God in your mercy …

*Pilgrim and all present:* Hear our prayer.

*Minister:*

Bless the parents of *(name)* and *(name)* and other family members affected by this change. Grant them wisdom in their continuing relationships, and comfort in their sadness. God in your mercy …

*Pilgrim and all present:*

Hear our prayer.

Minister:

Bless the friends of *(name)* and *(name)*. Give them your grace in the continuing relationship. God in your mercy …

*Pilgrim and all present:*

Hear our prayer.

**Lord's Prayer** *(said together)*

*Minister:*

God bless you in this new direction for your life.
From all the trouble may you grow in wisdom;
from all the tears and sorrow may you grow in compassion;
from this ending, may you know God's new beginning.
The blessing of the Living God
rest upon you and remain with you,
now and always.
Amen

Chris Polhill

# A liturgy for laying down and letting go

**Opening responses:**

As Columba laid down his books
and the security of a monastery
SO WE LAY DOWN WHAT IS PAST
AND LOOK TO THE FUTURE.

As Aidan and Cuthbert let go
and travelled hopefully on
SO WE LET GO HURT AND PAIN
AND TRAVEL WITH HOPE.

As Hilda changed direction
and relinquished cherished plans
SO WE LEAVE BEHIND FAMILIAR PATHS
AND TAKE NEW STEPS INTO THE UNKNOWN.

**Song**

**Prayer of confession:**

Merciful God,
for the things that we have done that we regret,
FORGIVE US.

For the things that we have failed to do that we regret,
FORGIVE US.

For all the times we have acted without love,
FORGIVE US.

For all the times we have reacted without thought,
FORGIVE US.
For all the times we have withdrawn care,
FORGIVE US.
For all the times we have failed to forgive,
FORGIVE US.

For hurtful words said and helpful words unsaid,
for unfinished tasks
and unfulfilled hopes,
God of all time,
forgive us.
and help us
to lay down our burden of regret.

**An act of contrition:**

*People are invited to write what they wish to lay down in their lives on a piece of paper, and to place it at the foot of a cross, or in a boat to be launched forth, or in a rubbish bin to be burnt, etc.*

*Alternatively people could be invited to place a lit candle by a symbol of new beginnings (a sandal, keys, an A-Z, a book open on a fresh page ...); or be invited to sow seeds of hope in a central pot.*

**Reading (Dandelion clock):**

Hope is a dark elusive child
curled in the womb
cradled in our arms.
It can be lost,
disappear,
blown on the wind like a dandelion clock.

Its going,
its ebbing away
leaves us
grieving,
empty,
hopeless.

'But' is a hopeful word.

But even as the gossamer
powder puff
disintegrates,
the seeds are carried
to cling to distant crevices.
As it recedes
it reseeds
to grow again.

God, giver of peace,
grow hope within and around us.
God of steadfast love,
never leave us hopeless.

A time of silence for reflection

Litany of letting go:

I let go:
window and door
house and home
memory and fear.

I let go the hurt of the past
and look to the hope of the future.

I let go
knowing that I will always carry
part of *my past/of you* with me,
woven into the story of my life.
Help *me/us*, Christ, *my/our* brother,
to softly fold inside
the grief and the sadness,
to pack away the pain
and to move on;
taking each day in your company;
travelling each step
in your love.

Blessing:

Pilgrim God,
our shoes are filled with stones,

our feet are blistered and bleeding,
our faces are stained with tears.

As we stumble and fall
may we know your presence
in the bleeding and the tears
and in the healing and the laughter
of our pilgrimage.

Kate McIlhagga


## Who will cast the first stone?

Who will cast the first stone?
The stigma of divorce still encircles my head, many years on,
like a crown of thorns;
the pain still pierces my side too,
where knives of unfaithfulness and abandonment
were once twisted in my heart;
and my body is bent low and weak
from carrying the burdens thrust upon my dejected shoulders.
Searching within hallowed walls I sought protection,
but within those walls criticism abounds
where guilt and blame are placed firmly at my feet.
For I was the one who did not, at first, forgive.
I am the leper of society within the family of the Church.
No longer a wife – yet not single or widowed –
who am I to expect equality?
They say I brought into my life my own misfortunes
because I did not turn the other cheek when the pain was great,
and I am told: 'God hates divorce.'

Yet Jesus accepts me, for he understands and bears my sin.
He forgives my weaknesses and loves me as I am.
So why can't you?
Why do you make me feel inadequate and inferior
when I feel so vulnerable already,
when I resist giving or accepting love
because I am afraid to love or trust again?
Don't you know my pain cries out for relief

and my body yearns to be held
and comforted in my loneliness and sorrow?

And so I stand, exposed to all who whisper behind hands,
'She's divorced, you know!'
And again I ask –
who will cast the first stone?

Christine Green

## Bring light out of darkness

Loving Spirit,
we pray for those whose experience of marriage
has proved too painful,
and where bitterness and hurt have been felt.
Bind the wounds and soothe the scars
that people have inflicted on each other,
and in your time and according to your ways
bring light out of darkness.
Amen

James Curry

## Grandpa's lament

I pray for God to bless
the child I once held,
now far away.

Are those little hands that once grasped my finger
full-grown and roughened by work?

Is that little face that creased in giggles
now shaved or bearded or acne-marked?
Custody battles long since fought and lost,
access rights now surrendered
and expense and distance
make my dreams impossible.

I'll never see the inherited likeness,
the family nose and chin.

Somewhere far away he lives
and, I hope, loves and is loved.

I pray for God to bless
the child I once held.

John Butterfield

# A litany of assurance following an abortion

*Incorporating Luke 3:22, Romans 8:31–39 and Luke 8:48 (NRSV)*

*A:*

O God, I have been so afraid. My world can seem chaotic and I sometimes feel all alone. I have faced difficult choices and needed you.

*B:*

I join with other people of faith in believing that regardless of whatever decisions you have made or will make, the caring support of your religious community, family and friends should always be yours.

*A:*

O God, I have been confused. It's hard to know what is right and what is wrong. Life is so unfair.

*B:*

God says: 'Know that you are my Beloved Daughter in whom I delight. If I, your God, am for you, who is against you? It is I, your God, who justifies, and my judgement is far more in your favour than all the unfairness of life.'

*A:*

O God, I have been brought up to think certain things were true: to revere life, to work for good. I feel I have disappointed you, other people and myself. I feel like such a failure.

*B:*

Who is to condemn? Only Christ Jesus, who descended into hell and rose again, to demonstrate that all the hells we go through, or put ourselves through, do not have the final word. There are no final words with God, only new words of assurance, grace and hope.

*A:*

O God, sometimes I just feel so bad. I feel myself separated from you and your desire for me in my life.

*B:*

Who will separate us from the love of Christ? Will hardship, or distress, or persecution, or famine, or nakedness, or peril, or sword, or abortion? No, in all these things we are more than conquerors, through Christ who loved us.

*A and B:*

I am convinced that neither death, nor life, nor angels, nor rulers, nor things present, nor things to come, nor power, nor height, nor depth, nor anything else in all creation, will be able to separate us from the love of God in Christ Jesus our Lord.

**Blessing:**

*B asks permission to lay their hands on the head of A.*

B:

Daughter, your faith has made you well; go in peace.

Lindsay Louise Biddle

# Parting

*Bits of a liturgy – choose what fits.*

God watches over our nights and days:
GOD IS WITH US NOW

God watches over our comings and goings:
GOD IS WITH US NOW

God watches over our meetings and partings:
GOD IS WITH US NOW

God is always with us:
GOD WATCHES OVER US WITH LOVE

**Prayer (Where we're at):**

We've messed it up, God,
we've lost it
and we're sorry …

A lot of people got hurt,
family, friends, the children,
and both of us.

It was good between us, God,
but not any longer.
It won't work, God,
we've talked it through,
we've cried together and alone,
we need to let each other go.

**Taking off the rings:**

Before you, and in the presence of family and friends,
we take from each other the rings that bind us …

*A to B:*

I take this ring off your finger.
You are no longer bound to me:
I let you go.

*B to A:*

I take this ring off your finger.
You are no longer bound to me:
I let you go.

*Said by someone present:*

A and B, you are no longer bound to each other.
You are free to lead a new life.

*A and B to their children:*

We are still your parents.
We love you.
You are not to blame for our separation.
Whatever happens we will find ways to care for you and love you.

We give you our rings
as a sign that you were born out of our love
and as a promise that we will go on loving you.

*Said by the wider family and friends to A and B:*

We know that you are no longer happy together.
We acknowledge that your relationship is over.
We wish you well as you go your separate ways.
We will stay in touch with you and support you as we are able.

*Said by the family and friends to the children of A and B:*

We love you.
We will not stop loving you.
We will find ways to be there for you when you need us.
We still love you and your mum and dad.

*Said by the congregation:*

We love you.
We will not stop loving you.
We want to support you and your children in your new lives.
We will pray for you.
We are here if you need us.
Please don't be afraid to ask.

A statement:

God is loving.
God is always loving.
Whoever we are,
whatever we've done,
wherever we go,
God is always loving.

A blessing:

Go now, into a new life.
May God the Maker bless you with wonder.
May God the Son bless you with love and justice.
May God the Holy Spirit walk with you into newness of life.
Amen

Ruth Burgess

## For the future

I remember a divorce ceremony I conducted once. I had conducted the wedding of the couple a year or so before, but things hadn't worked out, and they had decided to separate. We talked it through, and they agreed to having a very simple ceremony, in the open air as it happened, on a very stormy afternoon, when the elements seemed to echo the feelings that we had all been having. I can't remember the exact form of the service – there were just the three of us – but I do remember that it involved some words about letting go, the giving back of the rings, and a wee prayer for the future of all of us.

Somehow, it all just felt like the right thing to do – and that God was honouring them both as they sought to make sense of how things had gone, not as they would have hoped, of course, but nevertheless keeping hold of their care for each other and for their separate futures.

John Harvey

## God of our desire

God of our desire,
you show us in so many ways
what it is to love.
You do not hide from us
the pain,
the loneliness,
the fear and the despair
that there can be.
But neither do you withdraw from us
the joy,
the happiness,
the fulfilment and the certainty
that love brings.
Be with us through the times of shadow,
when we experience bleakness and lostness,
and save us from bitterness.
Show us the love that exists in new and different ways,
even in the shadow.
These things we pray,
through Jesus Christ,
the embodiment of love.
Amen

James Curry

# Home

# Prayers and symbolic actions for moving into a new home

Gathering words:

*Spoken by the person whose new home is being celebrated:*

Welcome to this place I am making my home.
Welcome to this place I am learning to love.
Welcome to my new home.

IN THE JOY AND WELCOME OF HOSPITALITY,
IN THE EXCITEMENT AND ADVENTURE OF MAKING A HOME,
IN THE VULNERABILITY AND RISK OF CREATING NEW SPACE,
WE GREET YOU IN THE NAME OF HOLY WISDOM.

A litany of keys:

*Members of the group are invited to pick up keys, or to hold their own keys, as they share their own stories or memories of moving into a new home. Then the following words are said:*

In the keys that unlock the door to the adventure and risk of a new home,
the excitement of moving into new space;
in the door that opens into new jobs and responsibilities,
taking charge of bricks and mortar, wood and glass:
WE LOOK FOR THE HOPE OF WISDOM.

In the keys that unlock the door to welcome and hospitality,
and a space to grow and flourish;
in the door that opens into comfort and safety,
a place of protection and refuge:
WE FIND THE PRESENCE OF WISDOM.

In the keys that unlock the door to planning colours and shaping space,
making a place of warmth and beauty;
in the door that opens into shared meals,
friendship and the creation of a place of flourishing:
WE EMBRACE THE LOVE OF WISDOM.

A litany of welcome:

*Members of the group are invited to place flowers in a vase, as they share what makes a welcoming space for them. Then the following words are said:*

For the welcome of colour and light,
warmth, safety and comfort,
PRAISE BE FOR THE GIFT OF HOSPITALITY.

For the welcome of food and drink,
a table set, a chair pulled out,
PRAISE BE FOR THE GIFT OF HOSPITALITY.

For the welcome of frayed edges,
the messiness of joining in,
PRAISE BE FOR THE GIFT OF HOSPITALITY.

For the welcome of books and plants,
music and a comfy chair,
PRAISE BE FOR THE GIFT OF HOSPITALITY.

For the welcome of a friendly smile,
a hand stretched out in greeting,
PRAISE BE FOR THE GIFT OF HOSPITALITY.

Jan Berry

## Blessing at the dinner table

Lord Jesus, you enjoyed gathering around a table with others,
not just for the special occasions
but also for the simple, everyday times.
You shared food, words of wisdom and laughter,
told stories and heard news of how your companions spent their days.
In breaking bread, you nourished love.

We ask your blessing upon our table,
and upon those who sit round it.
Bless our eating and our drinking,
our conversation and our listening to each other;
bless those who prepared and served the food,
and those who must do the clearing and washing-up.

Let this be a place where guests feel welcome
and all enjoy the riches of your creation;
may this be a place where love blossoms and is deepened,
where families gather to share with each other,
where friendships are renewed and strengthened.

Above all
let this be a place of laughter and joy,
of cheer and happiness,
where your goodness is glimpsed
and your kindness given thanks for.
Amen

Simon Taylor

## A garden blessing

O Jesus, who delighted in the beauty of flowers
and the songs of the birds,
bless this garden today and always.

May gentle showers water the plants,
warm sunshine encourage their growing
and the good earth nourish them.

Give joy and smiles to those who tend this place;
may all that is here delight and stimulate our senses,
and through this garden may we learn
to know more of your loving kindness
and to tend your whole creation with care and respect.
Amen

Simon Taylor


## Wanaki *

Bless this home, Lord,
the rooms, the hearth, the music, the voices.
Bless this doorway and all who come and go.
May they feel the welcome of Christ.

Bless this kitchen and all who cook, chop and serve here.
Bless this table and all the food heaped upon it.
Bless those who eat here and
bless all friends with warmth and trust.

Bless these beds and all who sleep in them.
May they rest in the knowledge of your abiding peace.

Bless this doorway
and all who step out into the night air.
May they pause beneath the stars,
sensing the great mystery of your presence.

Judy Dinnen

* Wanaki is the name of a friend's house.

## A last look back

Across this threshold feet have tromped – shoes off at the door, gear dumped to be sorted through after a shower and a rest; across this threshold groceries have been humphed, treasures have been carried, news has been handed on, and gossip.

Across this threshold, friends have come and gone. If you stand and listen, they still whisper into the silence around us, offering their blessings as you leave. Laughter and love is embedded in these walls, memories have sunk deep into the framework. You've packed away your things, and we take a last look back …

Journeying God,
love has held this house and made it a home.
Thank you for all the wise voices
and outrageous laughter
and secret shared whispers
that have filled this space and made it sacred.

Thank you for the ordinary moments
that became hours, days, years here –
all building blocks in life together.

Peace upon this house,
peace upon this family *(names)*,
peace upon those who will trudge and laugh
and live inside this threshold
from today on.

As those who leave close the door,
bless to them all the love they take along with them,
not packed away in boxes,
but folded into the fabric of their lives.
Amen

Sally Foster-Fulton

# The last return of the prodigal

I'd be the first to admit
he wasn't much of a pet.
I only took him in because his owners were moving away
and couldn't take him with them.

Once here he decided that he'd had enough of humans.
He'd never come when he was called,
he'd turn up for meals
if he felt like it,
sneer and snarl at me
(I can't ever remember hearing him purr)
or, if he felt inclined,
scratch and bite.

I still have the scars from the time
I tried to put him in a cat box
to take him to the vet.

But when he went missing for three days
I was worried.
I searched the garden and nearby streets,
asked the neighbours if they'd seen him.

Then one evening I found him lying in the drive,
hardly able to move,
obviously dying.
I wrapped him in a blanket and put him in his bed.
Characteristically he staggered out
and hid under a bookcase,
and twenty minutes later
he was dead.

I was grateful that the prodigal
had at least wanted to come home to die.

Brian Ford

## Blackstone's journey

Loud, persistent protests
as we set off from St Ives
on the long journey to the Western Isles;
the vociferous indignation
turning into intermittent pleas,
plaintive, compelling.

Out of his basket at every stop,
his elongated body sees all
through the windows.
Is he memorising his route home?
Every return to his basket
an unequal struggle.

Occasionally a paw stretches out,
scratches my arm – a reminder.
An overnight stop – no respite or rest
for driver or passenger.
The last lap – the ferry;
the movements and vagaries of the sea.

Snoring gently,
curled neatly into a ball,
a paw holding down an unruly tail;
comfortable on an uneven lap.
A picture of contentment,
settling into his new home.

Katherine Rennie

## Blackstone's love

Lying in bed,
feverish and out of sorts,
a sudden weight on my feet:
Blackstone has joined me.
Purring softly he curls up,
his body warm against mine;
here to share my misery,
to keep me company,
to watch over me.
His way of showing love.

Katherine Rennie


## Toby

Three times I drove past the door,
and three times I simply couldn't bring myself
to open it and carry her inside.

'But she's tired.
Her heart is finished.
You're not doing her any kindness,'
they kept on telling me,
and of course, I knew that what they were saying
was perfectly true.

But the thought of ending her life
was too much for me to handle:
the idea of her death,
and doing without her,
too difficult to embrace.

The well-worn arguments went round and round and round.
'What right do I have to choose the very moment?'
'She does not possess the power to object or refuse.'
'Where is my authority to make this final, fatal decision?'
'Ignorant and unaware,
if she knew what were being suggested,
would she consent and agree?'

'She's only a dog.'
I could easily have punched him.
'You can get another one,' said someone else.
It made me feel sick to the pit.
They didn't understand.
They had never been there.
They had never experienced the reality.
She was my loving companion,
my most forgiving friend,
the apple of both my eyes.

But it had to be done:
movements more painful;
vomiting more frequent;
hearing absent, and sight all but gone;
a leaky heart;
the obvious restlessness;
and now weak groans of discomfort
from deep inside.
The time had come:
the time for death.
It had to be done.

***

It was quick, it was gentle, it was kind
(or so I kept on telling myself).
As the needle went in,
I held her warm little body tightly.
The muscles relaxed,
and power departed,
and the heart stopped beating.
She sank onto the table and lay there lifeless,
and I tickled her ears,
and I made loving noises
as tears fell on her head.

***

From out of nowhere –
it struck me with all the force of a tidal wave.
I knew I'd be upset,
but never for a single moment did I anticipate
the gutting grief would be as intense and painful
as experienced now.

Uncontrollable sobbing.
A whole night without a wink of sleep.
Heart ripped in two, soul tormented, internalised writhing,
self-reproach and feelings of guilt.
What joy can be left?

Family is understandably concerned.
Wife suggests doctor.
'Don't be stupid!' the terse and dismissive reply.
Friend contacted, and arrives posthaste bearing whisky.
(True friends usually know exactly what to do!)
The next day, summoned daughter makes well-intentioned suggestions:
'Distraction therapy, a change of scene, we're going on an outing:
Christmas shopping – so let's get cracking, and put on your coat.'
But memory of it now is scarily absent;
coffee and bacon rolls in café erased from thought and mind.

***

So this is the grief I've heard them talking about.
And this is the nature of loss and unbearable pain
which others have known.
This the twilight zone when absence of happiness
is a torturing reality.
And this is the black-dog day
when no one has a right to say:
'She was only a dog.'

***

Can there be healing?
Will time make it better?
Can there ever be total mending and perfect repair?
For still I pine for her.
Still I ache to feel her sitting on my lap.
Still I wish I could touch those soft, brown ears
and look into those faithful brown eyes,
and witness the stump of a tail wagging vigorously
in unconditional acceptance.

It's true that passing time
has removed something of the sting and much of the sharpness.
But not for a minute can I ever believe
that the healing will be total and complete.

Glendon Macaulay

## Emptiness

The soft dark body no longer
dominates my bed.
Silence permeates every
corner of my home.
No intermittent thuds,
well-balanced crash-landings
from different launch pads.
No persistent complaints
at delayed meals or unsatisfactory food.
No pained looks from a cosy curled-up ball
at my late homecomings.
I miss him terribly.

Katherine Rennie


## All this stuff

There are very few spaces in my garden,
which is difficult when I want to plant something.
There are very few spaces on my bookshelf,
which is difficult when I acquire new books.
And as for the cupboard in the hall – don't go there!
All this stuff …
It's my home!

Ruth Burgess


## Amazing

Eating the fruit and vegetables I have grown
is amazing,
worth the battle with wily magpies,
chomping caterpillars
and fat slimy slugs

Eating the fruit and vegetables I have grown
is amazing –
and tastes so good.

Ruth Burgess

# Work and unemployment

## Starting a new job

God, thank you for this new beginning!
Thank you for the excitement and anticipation of a new start.
Thank you for the opportunity to use and develop my gifts.

Help me not to bring too much baggage,
to let go of past disappointments, failures, or sense of injury.
But help me to remember what I've learned,
and give me confidence to draw on my experience.

God, I pray for the people I'll be working with:
May we encourage each other and work well together,
learning and laughing and growing through the tasks we share.

God help me to begin anew,
confident in your love,
and trusting in your promise of hope.
Amen

Jan Berry


## A blessing on a new workplace

God, who lives and breathes in all we do,
we ask your blessing on this place of work.

May it be a place of comfort, health and safety,
with space and light, well-equipped
with all that's needed for thought and action.

May it be a place of communication,
where words are spoken to help and encourage,
where plans are shared and relationships forged.

May it be a place of inspiration,
where ideas and visions are sparked into life,
and dreams shaped into reality.

May the blessing of the creating God, who shapes the earth,
the blessing of the accompanying God, who walks with us,
and the blessing of the inspiring God, who breathes in and through us,
inhabit this workplace and surround all who use it.

Jan Berry

# Night shift

Six months after I graduated from university I got a job as a security guard. I pushed myself into the offices of the Wackenbush Security Company one afternoon, and was hired on the spot; was fitted with a scratchy-stiff uniform and handed a copy of their Rules and Procedures book.

Wackenbush would call me in the late morning – after I'd just worked all night – and ask me to do another night shift. I couldn't say no. I was broke and living back with my parents, sleeping in their basement.

I remember one morning: I'd been having a dream about Picasso. The two of us were sitting together at a little round table by the Seine, having a debate about the ultimate purpose and function of art. I was getting the better of him. Anaïs Nin was there, wearing a tight black dress, and dripping in silver jewellery and starlight. She was gazing across the table at me with her exotic, intelligent, big black eyes, her elegant long fingers stroking the stem and head of her glass of absinth …

I'd been dreaming about a life in Paris and of making love all night long with Anaïs Nin – maybe earning a mention in her famous diary – and was suddenly yanked up by my mother's voice: calling down the basement stairs that it was Wackenbush on the telephone asking me to do another night shift, in a plastics factory on the Puce River.

I worked in a plastics factory on the Puke River; in a supermarket, where I hid behind displays mostly, in case anyone, like old school mates, recognised me; in a fairground, where children stole my cop hat and teenagers challenged my authority; and during a postal strike, when I was spit on …

Finally they stuck me in some factory that made some kind of part for cars. Way out on the edge of town in the exiled, industrial badlands.

It was always night: You slept during the day, got up in the evening, and went to work for midnight. The only time you saw the sun was in summer. But since it was a perpetually dark night in my soul, I never saw it anyway. My depression eclipsed it.

When the birds started singing at the break of dawn, signalling that my night shift was almost over, I was glad – but wondered what it was they were so happy about. I couldn't see any rosy dawn on the horizon. Hope.

I'd gone to university to study English: the Romantics, the Beats – free-flowing spirits who didn't live by rules or clothe themselves in uniformity.

I'd taken courses in fine arts and in philosophy and religion, where I'd learned about great souls who had lived with 'authenticity': who had remained true to themselves in the midst of great hardship and suffering.

I'd been living in the rich world of literature: and was now earning minimum wage.

Around my neck hung a clock on a leather strap. There were seven stations in the factory which I had to visit on each of my hourly rounds. At each station, bolted into the concrete wall, was a little metal box with a lid, inside of which was a skeleton key on a chain. When I snapped this into the keyhole at the bottom of the clock, a mark was registered on the paper tape inside. In the morning, the security company and the factory owners read the tape to check I'd done all my rounds.

The heavy clock made my neck stiff, and the leather strap reminded me of a dog collar. So I walked round the factory with the strap wrapped round my wrist and the clock dangling. Another guard had advised to carry it in this fashion so that if I was ever attacked, I could use it as a weapon. 'It'll feel like you hit 'em with a ball and chain,' he said.

Walking the paths between the shadowy forest of machinery, to retrieve each of the seven keys from the seven boxes, I felt like I was trapped in some cruel fairy tale. Vats bubbled and steamed like miasmic bogs … I closed my eyes and prayed that one time I'd turn a key … and a magical passageway would suddenly open up – a doorway into another world.

Mostly, though, I felt trapped in a great beast. Even in the middle of the night the factory seemed alive – belching and groaning and farting; the stomach- and bladder- and bowel-shaped vats full of fumey, acidic chemicals that hurt my tired eyes.

Sometimes birds would get trapped in the factory. You could hear them – their distressed cries. You prayed that they would find a way out. An open window somewhere.

I found one dead once. Its beautiful colours, and intricate wonder of its wings, gone all sooty.

When I wasn't on my rounds, I sat stationed at an old metal desk, drinking strong, sweet tea from my thermos and reading books. In the bottom drawer of the desk, my colleague stashed porn, and the Rules and Procedures book.

The books I read were like windows of light:

In *The Tao Teh Ching*, I was in Tang-dynasty China, drinking tea in mountain huts with gentle monks, contemplating the eternal nature of the Tao. In *Moby Dick* I had jettisoned *'the damp, drizzly November in my soul'*, and was far away at sea – hunting the deep mystery of God with

Ishmael, Quequeg, and Ahab. In *The Tropic of Cancer* I had escaped absurd, humiliating, soul-destroying jobs with Henry Miller – and was living in Paris, in Montmartre (where Henry met, and repeatedly made love to, Anaïs Nin).

Books were my only friends. All my old schoolmates had moved away and started new lives – Life – in big cities. I'd graduated; and felt stillborn.

In the early morning, I was shit out through mud-spattered factory gates, while the workers were all swallowed up. In ones and twos … Young, hung-over guys, a few years older than me, hammering themselves with heavy drink every night. Old, ghostly men with DTs and brain damage, and wrecked eyesight and hearing.

The only thing good about working nights was that it kept me from running into my parents.

'At 19, I already had a house and family!' exclaimed my father, proudly, one night.

I explained to him that it was a different world now. I felt ashamed: I was 21.

'What different world?' he asked philosophically. 'Why does it have to be a different world?' he challenged. 'It's the same world.'

I didn't know what to answer. He just didn't understand.

I lay awake in my basement room, feeling like I was being slowly entombed. Fingers of sunlight reached in through the narrow window.

The only thing to do was to escape; to go back to school – forever … So I applied for a Master's course, and another student loan – and was accepted. It seemed like a chink of light. And I flew towards it with my sooty wings.

Neil Paynter

## You see their worth

Hear us, Lord, as we pray for those whose work is unrewarding,
who tackle basic jobs to keep life going
without a thank you, a pat on the back or any sign of appreciation –
without whom life would come to a standstill.

Glamorous folk would be robbed of glamour without them.
Big shots could not even step out of their houses
without the paths and roads they build and repair,
nor even have a house without their labour and skills.

You see their worth, Lord God.
To your eyes they sustain the fabric of the world.

Give us your eyes to see this,
and to honour and bless them.
Amen

Ian M. Fraser

## Collective dust

I have not been employed full-time since February 2009, and it has been a horrible period, to say the least. Not having a congregation to love and lead, to nurture and be nurtured by, has left me feeling empty, and wondering what my purpose in life is during this recession. Last week, as I considered where I would go to worship for Ash Wednesday, I found myself thinking of how I've been knee-deep in the Lenten reminders of temptation and wilderness and finitude for some time now. Ash Wednesday has always been one of my favourite services, but I decided to not even bother going.

Yet, when I woke up Ash Wednesday morning I had a great need to be amidst others in a congregation, to be broken and weary among other broken, weary, finite creatures. As I walked to a lovely Episcopal church for the noon service, I realised that what I've missed most is being part of a community. When I was a pastor, I spent many hours with men and women who had just been laid off, or feared being laid off, and they kept saying that they had no idea what they would have done without the support they felt at church. I finally really realised what they had meant. This is not to say that I have not had great support from family and friends, because they have been incredible, but I realised what I had been longing for was the day when I would again be emotionally attached to my brothers and sisters in a sanctuary day after day.

And while we stood to confess our sins in unison, I was overwhelmed with a feeling of empathy and of belonging to these people in this space. For we are all sinners and all broken. We are all formed from the same dust and breathe the same air. We all feel the pains of the same recession.

As we continued to confess our sins our voices grew stronger together, as our need for forgiveness and love was petitioned to the Throne of Grace. We stood in our own ash heaps begging the God of our lives to remember us, to forgive us, to sustain us – to revive us.

One by one we were marked with the ashes of our lives, reminded that we are but dust. Dust that was formed for a reason. Dust that was made alive with the breath of the Spirit. Dust that makes us equally vulnerable. Dust that is so beloved, the Word became flesh just to be among our dust.

*Thanks be to God for the dust of our lives*
*and for sending the Spirit to move us out of our own ash heaps,*
*to be reunited with our dusty, broken, beloved*
*sisters and brothers.*

Ashley-Anne Masters

## Wet and dry

People drip money these days,
those who have it,
they positively ooze consumer confidence,
it leaks from every tailored orifice
in sodden, saturating streams
of having.
These are wet people, if you like,
moist, poised,
lush, verdant, oily
people,
they lubricate the wheels
of economic
obesity.

People live in boxes these days,
those who haven't,
they beg for change from faceless crowds
on dusty streets of arid hopelessness

and smoulder inside their hollow smiles
with studied subservience
and conditional courtesy.
These are dry people, if you like,
desert dwellers
they scratch a living from the parched earth
of swallowed pride
and economic
necessity.

The rationale, of course, is familiar
if flawed:
the wet work,
the dry don't want to,
wealth
trickles down
wet to dry,
have to haven't,
the water flows,
the garden grows,
the status quos,
the cycle unbroken.

But, I'm not convinced,
are you?
Growth,
wealth,
prosperity,
patronage,
charity:
this model perhaps
fuels the flames of revolution,
this model perhaps
sows the seeds of environmental annihilation,
this model is not
sustainable.

Pete Anderson

## Not working

When hopes and dreams meet repeated rejection,
when years of education and training seem worthless,
when qualifications litter the road to nowhere:
God of our doing and being,
give hope and vision.

When jobs and relationships crack under the strain,
when daily activity is stress and pressure,
when the load of work is too much to bear:
God of our doing and being,
give healing and peace.

When purpose and identity fall into the chasm of unemployment,
when there is no longer a structure to the day,
when gifts and skills acquired over years seem redundant:
God of our doing and being,
give meaning and a sense of worth.

When the computer is switched off and activity ceases,
when the tools of the trade lie idle on the work bench,
when the calendar is blank of meetings and appointments:
God of our doing and being,
give rest and refreshment.

Jan Berry


## In the days

In the days
when there is
no paid work

In the days
when no one
is willing to hire me

In the days
when the system
grinds me down

Remind me God
you love me
and need me.

Ruth Burgess


## Day in

Day in
Day out
No money
No meaning

Day in
Day out
No security
No strength

Day in
Day out
No work
No warmth

Day in
Day out
God breathes
God listens

Day in
Day out
God loves
God loves me.

Ruth Burgess

# Prayers of intercession at a time of economic crisis

*Individuals or situations could be named in the spaces between the intercessions, and/or there could be a symbolic action: lighting a candle, placing nails or paperclips in a bowl …*

Let us pray for those who have lost their jobs,
are struggling with economic hardship
and trying to build a pattern for their days:
LOVING GOD, GIVE STRENGTH AND HOPE.

Let us pray for those who are fearful,
apprehensive about the future
and anxious about the loss of work and livelihood.
LOVING GOD, GIVE STRENGTH AND HOPE.

Let us pray for those working under pressure,
coping with increased workloads and fewer colleagues,
struggling to maintain an effective service.
LOVING GOD, GIVE STRENGTH AND HOPE.

Let us pray for those affected by cuts in services,
vulnerable people losing help they relied on,
left to struggle with illness, abuse or poverty.
LOVING GOD, GIVE STRENGTH AND HOPE.

Let us pray for those making decisions,
managers and policy-makers faced with hard choices,
looking to act with wisdom and integrity.
LOVING GOD, GIVE STRENGTH AND HOPE.

Let us pray for our society,
for increased compassion for the vulnerable
and a sense of justice in the places of power.
LOVING GOD, GIVE STRENGTH AND HOPE.

Jan Berry

# Health and caring

## After a heart attack

O Risen Christ,
you have put your ear to my heart
both when I prayed and when I doubted.
You know well the rhythm of its beat,
its strength, its weakness,
and when it scarcely beats at all.
You know well what I fear and question,
what I long for and need.
Great Heart of my own heart, whatever befall,*
may the strong pulse of your loving heartbeat
revive me,
strengthen me,
cheer me,
and rekindle my own
for you,
for me and mine.
Amen

David Hamflett

*\* This line was taken from Mary Byrne's hymn 'Be Thou my vision'.*

## As I bathe your body

*For Luca, living without the use of his legs*

As I bathe your body
help me to understand what it is to accept
the love of another,
to be open to others,
to be vulnerable,
for I keep others at a distance,
but you let us, every day, care for you.
Teach us to be as gentle with ourselves
as we are with you.
And may we be as patient with others
as you are with us.

Fiona van Wissen

## No words necessary

*For Ricky, a young man of very few words*

Your smile speaks louder than my words.
Your laughter lights the room.
And your seizures wound the depths of my heart.
You will never tell me your secrets
but your heart beats with the most beautiful song
that I will ever hear.

Fiona van Wissen


## Frequency

'I got to know him,' she said,
'as I went for all those operations.
There were so many.'
'We met,' he said, 'during her treatment.
Something changed.
We'll always be together now.'

We get joined up
when one wields or wars
on another's behalf.
Gathered up at the end of every day,
these we carry with us,
too hurt to manage alone,
somehow we are responsible
for them.

What gladness to receive
such wounded colleagues in the fight,
to have companions who know our story so well
they can tell it as their own.

See how each carries the other,
badged by honour in the struggle,
in deep understanding of the hurts,
each ever-seeking for the other
healing, wholeness and love.

Karen Reeves

## A carer's prayer

Compassionate God, you understand the burden of care that I carry.
You know that I do this as an act of love,
but you also know how difficult it is for me at times.
And I can be honest with you.

When I am at the end of my patience,
grant me a breathing space.
When I want to shout and scream with frustration,
open the safety valve that I need.
When I am so tired that I cannot think straight,
grant me that essential spark of energy that I need to keep me going.
When I cannot bear to watch the pain,
keep that agony from showing in my eyes.
When I long for a merciful death for this one I love,
hold me and grant me peace.

Dear God, help me to keep working and loving
until this suffering is over.
Amen

Marjorie Dobson


## God of the night-time

God of the night-time,
sharing our pain, our tears and our struggle,
draining the cup of what it is to be human,
you watch with us.

God of the night-time,
sharing our fears, our prayers and our restlessness,
measuring the road between living and dying,
you watch with us.

God of the night-time,
sharing the questions we never dare ask you,
yearning in us for the light of your glory,
you watch with us.

Ruth Burgess

## On living with times of illness and times of remission

There are two kingdoms:
one you enter without choice
each time illness finds you,
the other you find again once health returns.

Help me to take my place in each
with dignity and grace;
teach me acceptance, not shame,
for weakness of mind and body.

Remind us we always need the support of others
and to offer our support to those in need.
In times of illness and in times of health
may we know the grace of God
and know we are beloved children of our Creator.

Fiona van Wissen

# Moments of our days

## The gift of this day

Lord God, in the gift of this day,
help me to do and be
what you look for from me
in the life you entrusted to me.

Ian M. Fraser

## Jesus, my companion

Jesus, my companion, who walks with me on my way,
open my eyes to see you in the face of my neighbour,
open my ears to hear you in the voices around me,
open my mind to know you through your Word,
open my arms that I may embrace you,
open my heart that I may love you.
Amen

Travis Poling

## Reflections on a train journey

Perhaps we should see life more like a train journey:
as we bump along, the landscape reveals itself to us.

Something of interest flashes into view –
a chalk horse, a well-tended garden, a castle on a hill, a family at play …
We look with interest,
drawn, captivated for that moment,
but then all too soon
the embankment hides it from us
and it is gone,
left far behind us
as we continue on our way.

We cannot hold on to the moment,
we cannot stay there with it;
however much we might like to linger
the train moves on.

Lord, help me not to live in the past
but to celebrate the present
and anticipate the future that together
we are moving towards.

Simon Taylor


## The Golden Arches

I often find it a contradiction that McDonald's exists in many hospitals. While a Big Mac and fries is great comfort food, it isn't the healthiest option. However, in the hospitals where I've served as a chaplain, I have sometimes found those Golden Arches to be a gateway to holy ground.

I've shared a communion of chicken nuggets and Sprite with a family outside the ICU.

I've taken a McFlurry to a teenage boy who was having a horrible day – after finding out he'd be in hospital for another 4 weeks.

I've taken a large 'real Coke' to a grieving mother who, when I'd asked what she needed in that moment, had responded: 'I need a real Coke and a funeral service – but I need the Coke first.'

I've shared biscuits and coffee with the children of an 88-year-old woman while we sang 'Morning has broken', as their mother died just as the sun was coming up.

I've taken Fruit and Yogurt Parfaits to ER nurses after a long trauma in the small hours of the morning.

I've met family members of patients standing in line at McDonald's, and they've shared all kinds of emotions and thoughts they couldn't share in front of their loved one.

McDonald's isn't that healthy for our arteries but I believe it's sometimes good for our souls. So, the next time you do something outside of your comfort zone, or offer care to a friend, or have had a hard conversation, or take a family member to a doctor's appointment, drive on through the Golden Arches and get a little soul food in the form of chicken nuggets, a 'real Coke' or a McFlurry. Being all grown up takes an awful lot of bravery some days, and you're never too old for a Happy Meal.

Ashley-Anne Masters

## Signs of God

*(Tune: Bard of Armargh/Streets of Laredo)*

What signs of God's glory are seen in the city,
hemmed in by the buildings of concrete and ore?
For we cannot tread the rich earth on hard pavements,
or hear the sheep bleating above the cars' roar.

Yet still we can scour the sky for God's patterns,
or notice a flower blooming on some waste ground,
and glimpse in a spiderweb shimmering dewdrops,
for in the unnoticed our Creator is found.

We see God behind the sad eyes of a vagrant,
hear God in the cry of a child who's afraid;
and in work-worn features of stressed city slickers,
our God reaches out to the world that he made.

So help us to notice, great God of Creation,
your handiwork traces in country and town;
in city or wilderness, may we discover
that your living presence is always around.

Carol Dixon


## The journey

*Thump, jump, flutter,* goes my heart, *here we go again,* goes my head – am I going to pass out? Panic. I can't do it! *Oh, do shut up,* I tell myself.

I stop and take some Rescue Remedy.

I'm on a bus to take me to the metro station; then I'm taking a metro to go to the shops in the city of Newcastle. Most people, or so I think, can do this journey on automatic pilot, but not me. I have a phobia about travelling and I haven't been able to use the metro for seven years. So I've given myself a challenge to do this – and I'm terrified.

*Breathe slowly, deeply,* I tell myself … Phew, the Rescue Remedy is beginning to work.

I alight from the bus and walk up the steps to the metro station; my legs feel like jelly. My hands shake as I buy my ticket, my feet tell me I'm scared, my head tries to pretend I'm doing OK, as I look around at other people casually buying a ticket. *Where shall I sit?* I say to myself, looking around. I sit next to a woman of about my own age, travelling alone, who seems very calm. I smile and pretend to be OK.

The doors close – we're off: there's no going back now. Tyne Dock, Hebburn, Heworth pass by, picking up people and getting busy. *Breathe, breathe,* says my head to my heart, *don't panic, nearly there,* as daylight flashes across the Tyne, then underground again. *I'm doing well,* I tell myself, *next stop mine: get ready to alight.* Monument, I see in bold letters, and can't wait to stop. I proudly press the green light and step off. I've done it. I've arrived! Primark here we come.

Sarah Pascoe

## Cleveland Way haiku

*Inspired by walking the first half of the Cleveland Way, from Helmsley to Saltburn, August 2010*

*Sunday: Rievaulx Abbey*

Place of work and prayer
ancient stones warmed by the sun
peace is in the air.

*Monday: Helmsley to Sutton Bank*

Walking on cold lanes
watching gliders in warm sun
tea and cake at end!

*Tuesday: Sutton Bank to Osmotherley*

Cobwebs on wet trees
sun shining on heather moors
heading for the cross.

*Wednesday: Osmotherley to Clay Bank*

Honey-scented air
coast-to-coast walkers join us
on steep moorland climbs.

*Thursday: Clay Bank to Kildale*

Wind and sun on skin
hand-stones and moorland crosses
butterflies dancing.

*Friday: Kildale to Saltburn*

Moors and forest paths
blown away by wind and views
long wet stretch to coast.

*Saturday: Saltburn*

Space to rest and play
fish and chips at the seaside
castles in the sand.

Jan Berry

# From Caedmon's song

I sing you in the quiet and calm of dawn.
I sing you in the questions and controversies of morning.
I sing you in the answers and possibilities of afternoon.
I sing you in the conversation and debate during mealtimes.
I sing you in the resolution and relaxation of eventide.
I sing you in the warmth and depth of night.

Judy Dinnen

# Beloved God

Beloved God,
in the holy book help me to read You.
In the book of my life let me live You.
In the book of creation let me see You.
In the book of my neighbour let me love You.
Amen

Stephen Wright

# I need a new address book

I need a new address book –
my old one is falling apart,
full of alterations and amendments,
crossings-out, additions, deletions –
my friend in Taiwan has moved
eight times in the last ten years.

New partners, new addresses,
babies born, children leaving home,
divorces, separations, bereavements.
Couples have become singles.
Partners now living alone.
I pray for them in their loneliness and all the changes:
I know what they're going through.

And as I bring all these old friends before the Father
I hope they pray for me too.

Brian Ford

# A wee prayer for good times

God of generosity and grace,
within us, around us, beyond us,
at this time when our spirits are high, our health is good,
our life is fulfilling and the outlook is promising,
may we have the sense to keep our feet on the ground
and our hearts and minds open to the needs of those who are less fortunate.

Grant us humility in all things,
for these good times are a gift beyond our deserving.

May we take nothing for granted
and recognise that there will be times ahead
when we shall need the loving support and help of others.

In and through all the ups and downs of our lives and our dealings with all,
may we grow ever closer to you who are
the source of all goodness
and the ground and energy of all being.

Norman Shanks

## The dangers and grace of routine

Lord God, save us from the dangers of routine,
especially when we are young:
from playing safe, quenching the adventurousness of faith;
from expecting our needs to be met,
to be provided for as if it were our right;
from entering each day as if there were no strangeness and wonder
that we were given one more day to live, after the death of sleep;
from drawing breath without thanksgiving
that our lungs are attuned to the air;
from accepting the service of others without thought or appreciation
when we should be stirring ourselves to play our part;
from choosing comfort when there is work to do;
from seeking reassurance in activeness when we need time for thought;
for sticking with positions we hold when it is time to question them.

Lord God, make us thankful for the grace of routine,
especially when we are old:
that there is a place for our spectacles
where we can bring them into use and return them;
that there are days for different things so that we don't get muddled;
that there are pills to balance out-of-kilter parts of the body
and times to take them;
that the mobile library visits regularly on set days;
that people get to know our ways and allow for them.

Ian M. Fraser

# For self-examination

Am I offering back my whole life to God each day?

No other life anywhere in the world at any point of human history is the mirror of mine. Do I treasure its uniqueness, insist on space to be myself? …

Whatever other people think I should make of my talents and opportunities, am I open to learning the purpose for which God has given me this particular life; so that at the end of the day I will have played my part in rooting the Kingdom values where my life is set? …

My vocation is to be fulfilled in a family: of parents, brothers and sisters; or of partner and children; or of a small community of friends. Do I neglect them, or use them just when it suits me? Do I lay aside time really to belong, really to appreciate and nourish close, committed relationships? *'Faith, hope, love: these three. But the greatest of them all is love.'* How is my love expressed? …

I have not chosen my race or nation. Do I contribute to its life, supportively and critically? Do I make that contribution with an awareness, which I am ready to share with others, that all races and nations are called by God to belong to one community? Have I worked out a true proportioning of church-based and world-based commitments so that they instruct each other? …

Have I learned to say 'no' to requests which would swamp me? …

Am I prepared to be available in situations which I don't like facing, in which I could help people to tackle the challenges of life more creatively? …

*'So teach us to number our days that we may apply our hearts unto wisdom'* (Psalm 90:12).

*God the Lord,*
*every part of my life is a trust from you.*
*It is with my whole being that I am called to respond to that trust.*
*Save me from neglecting any of the assignments and relationships*
*that make up my life.*
*Save me from being overwhelmed –*
*my sufficiency is of you and not of myself.*
*At the end of the day have mercy on my soul;*
*and grant that none of those who have been tied in the bundle of life with me*
*may perish because of any defect on my part.*
*In Jesus Christ's name.*
*Amen*

Ian M. Fraser

## Blessed are ...

Blessed are the dog-walkers,
for they shall discover the kingdom's streets.

Blessed are the asylum seekers,
for they shall be a home for others.

Blessed are those who read to children,
for they shall plant seeds of wonder.

Blessed are those who weep for the homeless,
for they shall be shawled in God's grace.

Blessed are those who stock food pantries,
for they shall taste God's hope.

Blessed are those who bring in the marginalised,
for they shall be called bridge-builders.

Blessed are the faith-full foolish,
for they shall be called the clowns of God.

Thom M. Shuman

# We sleep into mystery

We sleep into mystery, Lord Christ, losing control of our lives, wandering in strange worlds of the imagination, defenceless against any horrors which may invade.

You who, wakeful for our good, laid aside your glory to become one of us, who slept through storm in a boat, trusting in the Father's unsleeping care, help us to gain a like faith in facing life's challenges.

You who refused dope to dull the agony of crucifixion, determined to be at one with every racked and tortured soul who died heartbroken, save us from complacency with our privileged lot, careless at the cost of which some of our necessities and luxuries are provided. Stir us to seek justice for all and pursue it, that we may share in that costly at-one-ment with all humanity which you chose.

We waken into mystery, Lord Christ, not knowing what a day will bring forth, what trusted relationships may turn sour, what temptations may get under our guard, what opportunities for witness and service may be missed. But we also waken to your unfailing love which speaks forgiveness and restoration to our faults and failures and which takes the wisp of smoke of our offerings and blows it into flame, the Spirit's flame encompassing it and enhancing its substance.

We waken to the mystery of life renewed beyond our power, of air prepared for lungs and blood pumping life through bodies which we did not design, of minds refreshed. We waken to trust placed in us beyond our deserving, to the loving kindness of family and friends, to those who continue to uphold us in prayer, to all who keep us journeying into the truth …

And when we sleep the last sleep, mystery of mysteries, wonder of wonders, we waken in the everlasting arms.

We give you glory, Lord Christ, which was yours to resign for our sakes and yours to reappropriate beyond your own last sleep of death. Waking and sleeping we look to you for life. Amen

Ian M. Fraser

# Being who I am

## Being who I am

What am I worth?
I have no grand title – Supervisor, Manager, Chief Executive.
I have no authority – no one comes and goes at my beck and call.
I have no powerful voice – others do not hang on my every word.
I have no job – society does not value me.

I am not defined by what I do,
but by who I am,
your child,
loved.

Janet MacDonald


## Songs of praise

The music is so beautiful –
soaring into the dimly lit vaulted roof;
the notes float pure and free
and hearts are moved
and grateful:
hearts are changed.

The music is so beautiful,
until disturbed and fractured
by discordant notes;
not floating, but scraping,
not rising, but …

Great God,
if you desire a people
filled with glorious worship,
songs of praise,
surely it would have been a small kindness
to let me sing
in tune!

Carolyn Morris

## Some people look at me

Some people look at me as if I'm not human.
It wasn't my fault that I was born like this.
But when you're not the same,
some people can't cope with that.
They bully, or call me names, or stare,
or play on my weakness,
knowing that I can't fight back.
Why are they so cruel?
Why is life so unfair?

God, do you love me?
Am I really made in your image,
as the kind and loving ones try to tell me?
Are they telling the truth?

I really need to know!

Marjorie Dobson


## Some people say

Now and again, some people say
I have a lovely smile,
that when I smile,
which isn't enough,
the world lights up.
Some people say
I smile with my heart.

Sarah Pascoe

## I found God in Bangladesh

I found God in Bangladesh:
in the outstretched hand of a child begging in the streets;
in the resilience of a rickshaw man working from dawn to dusk;
in the colourful, vibrant dresses of girls and women;
in the energy and ingenuity of street vendors
seeking out a living day by day;
in the quiet commitment of NGOs
working in slums, brothels, hospitals and villages;
in the woman living over a sewer,
hanging out her washing on a barbed wire fence;
in sitting at prayer with Muslims in a makeshift mosque;
in teaching a class of students – alive with questions;
in watching women dodging the traffic to sweep the streets
at five in the morning …

Coming home was a bit of a revelation –
not quite the surge of excitement I'd expected,
but wrestling in the wee small hours
with the poverty and richness of such a different culture,
and trying to make sense of it all.

Finding God … not in the big gestures,
but in small things:
the young boy who picked a water lily
and wove it into a beautiful necklace for me;
strangers at the railway station
who helped us find our coach and seats on the train
amidst the noise and chaos;
birdsong after a night of thunder and lightning and monsoon rain;
a brown tree frog sitting on my bed
on the morning after the storm …

That was the real homecoming:
finding God again in the little things,
no matter who we are
or where we are.

Katy Owen

## Andrew the runner

I have quite severe autism, a diagnosis which has tended to define and limit me all my life. I am hypersensitive to just about everything, especially sound, touch and bright lights. I react badly to many common foods and cannot take any medication. I have times of being tense and stressed, or frozen and stuck, and since the age of 30 have been surprised by grand mal seizures. My nervous system is disordered so I cannot speak with my voice, though I have learned to express myself on computers with voice output.

As a child, I would run, or bolt, very fast to clear my head or get away when distressed. But this running had to be discouraged, as it endangered my safety and nobody could keep up with me. I accepted that running was out though would still sometimes make short dashes. As an adult I have developed a very good life, including regular walks with a series of companion dogs. But I have missed the running.

About five years ago, one of my health professionals, who is a marathoner, suggested that raising my endorphin levels through running could improve my health and sense of well-being. Some running friends made time for me in their busy lives and we ran together occasionally. Then nine months ago, two new partners offered to support regular runs. We get out almost every weekday morning for up to 8 kilometres and I have competed in two races.

I love both the exercise and the companionship and wish I could run every day! I like walking very much as well, but the energy rush that happens when running is an entirely different peace that comes within me. After I had been running only a couple of months, I composed the following poem to express the joy I feel. Over the past five years, several other running poems have emerged.

### Andrew the runner, man of peace

Running is a way for me to go with my feelings.
I think it helps clear my head for good thinking.
Yes, running is an avenue to freedom for me.
It is a great way to make connections with new people,
and that connects me with myself more as well.

I feel like Andrew who runs,
not Andrew who is an autistic man.

I am free from the stress
of the sounds of home
and the hum of the world.

I just feel the sounds
of my own body and spirit.

Running is peaceful and calming for me.
I can free myself from all worries
and just run towards
the lightness of feeling
close to nature and God.

I feel a sense of being freed
from all things that restrict me.
I am running to me.
I feel so much better as a person
with the ropes of autism broken from me.

I am Andrew the runner.
I am Andrew who has hopes and dreams.
Andrew the runner,
now closer to being free and just me.

Running gives me a sense of peace,
which you can only achieve
through loving yourself
and the wonderful creation you are.
I am running towards this person,
Andrew the runner.

I am Andrew the runner.
I love feeling this peace.
I can only run faster and harder
to find the runner in me.
Then I will be at peace.

I am Andrew the runner.
I want to run fast and furious.
I am challenging myself to be
a man of full potential,
and that includes my peace.

I am running to me.
I am Andrew the runner.

Andrew Bloomfield (16 October, 2009)

## Who am I?

Who am I, Lord God, who comes to worship you?
Can the worship of such as I am be acceptable in your sight?
I see a face in a mirror. That's me.
I know how friends and family react to me. That's me.
But beyond all that what am I in your sight?
What do you make of me?
Do you accept joyfully the worship of such as I am?

I thought that if I abased myself before you, Lord,
you would approve.
It is a biblical thing to do.
The Psalmist said 'I am a worm and no man.'
Isaiah – the pot has no right to say to the potter
'Why have you made me thus?'
So I scraped round
searching for things to confess
which would make me
small, worthless and guilty.

But you, God the Lord, said 'Enough of this crap:
stand on your feet, hold your head high.
You are no worm. You are no mere clay pot.
You are my beloved child made in my image:
Grow up! Look like what you are!'

You put me right about myself.
Good for you, Lord.
Receive the thanks and praise of your chosen ones.
Amen

Ian M. Fraser

## Bodhrán*

The Corries started it really – this fascination with the bodhrán. They were on television one evening. Just what was that amazing drum they were playing?! Come on, drums are played upright, aren't they, not sideways on? What was *that*?! It was to be a half-forgotten memory.

Some years later, there was a photo of Christy Moore on the back of a Planxty album. Hey, he's playing one of those drums the Corries had! What's it called? A what? However do you pronounce that? The memory reawakened, and I heard and saw it played quite a bit after that. A fascination was rekindled.

A ministerial further training course many years later: 'What,' we were asked early on, 'would you like to do just for you, just for yourself, that you don't do already?' I heard myself say: 'Get a bodhrán.' The fascination was going to become more than just an idea.

And I did just that. I bought my first bodhrán. (I've bought much better ones since.) At last – at last. Let's go! It can't be that difficult to play … can it? Oh yes, it can! Frustration wasn't the word! Was I ever going to get even the beginnings of the hang of this?

Then, one day, something just clicked. I stopped thinking and trying too hard, felt the rhythm of the reel, and let go. Let the tipper dance! A beginning. More an instinctive player than a technical one, I've listened, watched – the top players are simply amazing and leave me open-mouthed – played, listened, watched, learned a few things, listened, learned, played some more. And keep listening, learning and playing. Trying to get the sound, the tone, the rhythm. Some days it just won't come, I just can't get it; other days I'm away.

The session, my musical pals, some tunes and songs and me with a bodhrán in my hands, and I'm as happy as Larry. Bliss! Heaven.

Iona Abbey: and we were going to play 'I will always bless the Lord' in the morning service, and send everyone out to 'Drowsy Maggie' afterwards. (By the way, Maggie was anything but 'drowsy' – unless it was a joke!)

'Ah! A bodhrán player! Any good?'

'Yes, he is actually.' Quite matter of fact.

No one had ever said I was any good before. Wow! Some years later I told the person who said that just how much her comment meant, and still means.

Iona Abbey again, and I'd just been playing bodhrán to Marty Haugen's fine hymn 'All are welcome' at the end of worship.

'How do you play *that*?' a wee girl asked as she walked past on her way out. Caught on the hop, I struggled for an answer.

'I don't know,' I said. 'I just do.' And I showed her a few things and let her hold and try the bodhrán.

Do they have sessions in heaven, do you suppose? Is there a band of angels there who can use a bodhrán player someday? I do hope so!

* *'Bodhrán' is pronounced 'bough' (as in the branch of a tree) 'rawn'. A tipper is the name for its stick, although some players play with their hands.*

David Hamflett

## Just as I am

I was born as a Down's Syndrome tot,
and I can tell you that's what I've got.

It's the way I am, I'm not complaining,
everyone's different, no need for explaining.

I'm maybe disabled, but I have to live with it,
even if I don't like it one bit.

Just as I am, Lord, that's how it is,
completely owing my life now to his.

There's nothing you can do to change it,
I'll always be like this –
I won't quit.

Karen Kinloch

## Down's Syndrome

I get up in the morning and I look through
the mirror, it just scares me, that I'm blue.

Everybody looks at me and they stare.
Am I just someone like a statue, that they glare?

I can't be like everyone else, it's not fair,
working night and day, up and down the stair.

Disabled I am, but I'm very witty,
clever also and sitting looking pretty.

There may be people who don't want to know me.
That's their loss, just let me be.

My hobbies are golf and swimming
and sometimes, if I'm in the mood, go slimming.

Being disabled like this cannot be helped at all,
after all I am human and not that tall.

One thing I know of all people like me,
well, it's good to know you care, you see.

Karen Kinloch

## Inconsistency

Each year an invitation comes
to join in the commemoration
of Holocaust Memorial Day.
We praise those people who
to save the Jews
smuggled them here or
wangled visas.
Now such acts
bring disapproval
and imprisonment.

Today's asylum seekers are not seen
as needing such assistance.
Perhaps because they come from further off?
Because they are not white?
Because their former way of life
is seen as poorer: so they come here to get a better life?
But some of them come from places where they had enough –
lived in better comfort than they can here.

Rebels in Libya are assisted,
we intervene to stop the persecution of civilians,
but Biafrans threatened our oil supply
so it was not right to help.
Those of us who were working there
and felt we could not leave
took risks.
We did not claim that as relief suppliers
we should be exempt from danger.
Some died – Mother Cecelia, Marj and Tarka,
pilots of airlift planes, a Red Cross team …

As one who was a refugee,
who ran before advancing troops,
who had to choose between
a box of books
or a bundle of firewood
when fleeing from Okigwi,
I know what leaving all behind can mean.

My cook went out to serve drinks of skimmed milk to people
streaming down the road;

but only those who had a mug or an empty tin could get it,
unless someone already served would lend their tin.

I understand how people fight over donated jumble –
old clothes, pots, pans, sheets and blankets.

Do you understand?

Anne Seymour


## Gracious friend

Gracious friend
and God of compassion,
we reach out to you for understanding
whilst hardly understanding ourselves.

We turn to you for eternal truths
yet can barely look ourselves in the eye
when our words are less than honest.

We ask that our open hearts be blessed by you
yet dither and deny
when your existence is questioned and challenged.

We take part in catastrophic wars
yet turn to you looking for peace,
and fail to understand when the war rages on.

We ask that poverty ends here, ends now,
yet look over our shoulder in horror
when a hand is held out in desperation.

God of our understanding,
help us see the real face:
ours and yours.

Help us see the real needs,
ours and theirs,
and help us catch a glimpse
of a world that can be.
Amen

Alma Fritchley

## Ordination

The shaft of sunlight penetrated the window.
I felt the warm light upon me.
I had hoped for this all my life.

The oil touched my hand.
I was anointed.
I was holy.
Set apart.

I had hoped for this all my life.

June Boyce-Tillman


## On becoming a church elder

I knew it, Lord, I knew it.
I knew they would ask me to become an elder.
And
I knew exactly what I was going to say:
'It's not my thing,
I'd be no good at helping run a church,
I won't do it.'
Then I heard you say,
quite clearly,
'Shouldn't that be my decision?
Of course you'd be no good at it,
totally inadequate is the phrase I'd use –
and I know you far better than you do.
But I'll be with you
and I am more than adequate.
So do it …
Please.'

Brian Ford

# Growing older

## Growing older

God, whoever, wherever, whatever you are …
(and even that 'you' doesn't seem right any more)
this growing old is a strange business –
a complex mixture of what is challenging and fulfilling,
and fortunately never boring:
there are always things to do, places to go, people to see.
Yes, there's maybe more time and the pace is a little easier than it used to be;
I've got better at saying 'no';
but I still don't think I've got my priorities quite right,
and in particular, I wish I was better at giving more time
to reading, reflection, listening to music …

And increasingly, mind and body show signs of aging:
the retrieval system isn't as good as it used to be,
energy levels have certainly declined,
back and legs grow stiff and sore too quickly.
I was never the most patient person,
and I suspect that's not improving.
But I've come to value family and friends more than ever.

What I really want to tell you (there it is again!) about
is the way some of the deep questions
are increasingly preoccupying my attention –
especially about you, God,
about life, and time and eternity, and about faith.
I've always been interested in this stuff, but now
I'm so aware I know 'less and less about more and more'.
And yet there's this paradox:
at the heart of all the peripheral doubts and uncertainties
(about Bible, church, etc)
and my awareness of the essential provisionality
of so many of our beliefs, structures and processes,
I am totally convinced that there is something true, beautiful, just and good.
In that I can trust; by that I can live.
I am grateful for the miracle and mystery of grace.

Norman Shanks

## Second life (prayer for a 50th birthday)

As I begin my second life
I remember the innocence and ideals of my youth,
loving the world,
working with others,
caring for children.
I carry all this into the future,
not resting but always seeking.
May I have compassion for those who follow behind –
the young, the inexperienced,
all who strive to live and find meaning.

May we all know
that there is always more life,
always more love.
There is always more.

Sandra Kramer

## Retirement

I wonder what that is! And when it will really start! I retired from my profession of Pharmacy in 1998 just before we left Redditch for Iona. After all, the nearest pharmacy to Iona is either in Tobermory (a boat ride and 60 miles away) or Oban (two boat rides and 37 miles away). Not much chance to practise there! So a new stage opened up in my life: the beginning of 'retirement'. It was probably the hardest job I had ever done, but I wouldn't have missed it for all the world! I had happily worked for six weeks as a volunteer on the island some years before, but nothing could have prepared me for the experience I had on Iona between 1998 and 2001 – the ups and downs, the people, the beauty of the island, the visitors, the Resident Group, the volunteers, working in the bookshop, so much to learn, so much to do and never enough hours in the day. Could this really be the start of my retirement?

After three amazing years it was time to return to the 'real world' and begin again in St Albans. Brian, my husband, to be minister of two United Reformed churches. And me? Well, perhaps this would be retirement? Or perhaps not! Two very busy and totally different situations, and a new beginning. At one church I hosted monthly manse coffee mornings; at the other I started a Traidcraft stall; at both I became one of the Sunday musicians; and having avoided eldership throughout my married life I found myself becoming an elder in both churches at once! I did find time to do one morning a week in the Oxfam bookshop. After Iona I had a special love of books and bookshops. And I also became a volunteer for Arthritis

Care, a cause close to my heart, leading self-management courses and enabling people to find advice and assistance. So it wasn't all church.

Then five years and many happy times later Brian retired. We thought long and hard about where. In the United Reformed Church you can retire anywhere except close to your last pastorate. Eventually we settled on Bristol, where both of us had been very happy in the 1970s, and where our elder daughter lives. We found a semi-detached house and gradually settled in. Perhaps this would be retirement? Two weeks after we arrived our daughter told us she was pregnant! The longed-for grandchild we thought was never going to be ours was 'on the way'. The excitement was enormous. Then we heard our other daughter was going to the House of Commons to receive an award for her work with Peace Brigades International in Guatemala. Would we go with her? Of course!

And what else? Well, just after we arrived I contacted Women's World Day of Prayer, as it is still called in England. I had always been involved in it, and wanted to know what was happening in Bristol. The Bristol chairwoman said, 'You don't happen to be a musician, do you? Our present one has to give up, and we are desperate!' So now I play for the Bristol area conferences and sometimes help with local services.

I was also welcomed with open arms by the South West region of Arthritis Care. I have managed to continue my interest in interfaith activities, which began when we were in St Albans. Having been fortunate enough to find a wonderful United Reformed church we have become very involved with that. And I also play the piano for services in a new Methodist Home that has opened near us, and for a branch of the Alzheimer's Society's 'Singing for the Brain' that meets in our church.

So *this* is retirement! My last five years have been pretty remarkable. A friend who had been trying to contact me was heard to say, 'You are as busy as ever you were when you were working.' My reply is: 'Ah, but now I am doing the things I choose to do!' Maybe not some people's idea of retirement, but most of the time it suits me fine!

*Living and loving God,*
*please help me to make the right choices,*
*to get my priorities right,*
*to know when to do and when to be,*
*to get the balance between sleeping, eating and working*
*and to always make sure that You are in the middle.*
*Amen*

Sheila Woodcock

## I'm new to this volunteering lark

I know, Lord, I know.
It's good for my humility.
The man who managed a large academic department,
directing the work of a dozen graduates,
is now spending his time cleaning out chicken sheds.
The one who set and marked A-level papers sat by thousands of students
is carrying cups of tea to people with learning disabilities.
I'm not the boss any more.
I'm the new boy who doesn't know the ropes,
the untrained volunteer
who has to ask the old hands for advice.
And yes, yes, you know all about humility:
You who made countless number of galaxies
knelt down and washed twelve pairs of smelly feet.

Brian Ford

## And shall we play bingo?

Retirement is theft.

It steals some of the best years of our lives. Often we allow those years to be stolen. Retirement is the opposite of discipleship. It is an act of ingratitude – an offence against God. It's a deceit – a confidence trick.

'When did you retire?' they asked solicitously.

'When I was sixty-five,' said the man with grey hair. 'Retirement age.'

'What do you do now?' they asked.

'Oh, I play golf once in a while,' he said.

'And I watch TV,' he added. 'I put my feet up. Do the crossword. After all, I'm sixty-eight now. An old age pensioner. At my time of life you need to take things easy.'

Really? Think about some people older than him: Sean Connery, naturalist David Attenborough or TV cook Mary Berry. Are they sitting back taking it easy?

If some of us find such people alarming, we will be disappointed to find the Bible offers little by way of consolation. In fact, God seems to delight in rubbishing the idea of a quiet old age. How old was Abraham when he set out on his great journey? Or Zechariah and Elizabeth, the aged parents of John the Baptist?

Of course, the Bible does sometimes reveal cases of people who retired. Jesus took early retirement from the timber trade and several of the disciples had recently retired from jobs in the fishing industry. Then there was Levi, who suddenly decided to retire from the well-paid financial services sector.

They retired – but did they play bingo?

God has spent years pouring into us wisdom and experience, knowledge and insight, faith and love. Does he have no task for us to do in His name? We who are in our later years have been given huge gifts. Gifts to be used in life-long discipleship. A servant calling which is the gift of life itself.

Is your body tired and aching? Get out of the house and walk; walk further tomorrow; sign up at a gym; go for a swim; do Pilates; take up yoga. Is your brain tired? Wake it up: join a house group, an Amnesty group, a Christian Aid group …

Become a campaigner. Challenge injustice. Go on political demonstrations. Read your newspaper (not a Tory one!) and pray your newspaper. Lobby your MP.

Be a rebel, as Jesus rebelled against sin and injustice. Get arrested, as he did. Grow old disgracefully – as he lived and died disgracefully. Believe in the spirituality of life: the spirituality of laughter. Love your enemy. Encourage the faint-hearted. Wear red socks.

Refuse to retire. Refuse to be categorised as old. Use the dynamic gift God is giving you in the sacrament of the present moment – no matter what the date is on your birth certificate; whether you are confined to a bed, a wheelchair or an iron lung.

If you can breathe you can serve.

Retired? Not a chance: you're too busy. In fact – you've hardly started living!

David Rhodes

## Future shock

Not long ago
I was as young as you are now.
It seems I only turned my head
and it turned back covered with snow;
and tall young people
look at me, as if to say:
'You must have been old forever and a day' –
but they were babies when I turned away.

Roddy Cowie


## Thank you God that nobody minds

Thank you God that nobody minds:
that I fall asleep in the afternoon,
that I think the 1980s were too recent be nostalgic about,
that I know nothing about current pop music,
that, given half a chance, I bawl out '60s rhythm and blues songs
at the top of my voice,
that I think Max Miller (who?) was the greatest stand-up comedian ever,
that I say thirty bob when I mean one pound fifty,
that I don't watch reality television,
that I'm not interested in football,
that I don't know the difference between an iPod and a Blackberry,
that I constantly forget people's names,
that I greet strangers in the street,
that I'm wearing odd socks and a jumper with holes in it,
that I've dripped soup down my shirt front,
that I'm not interested in fashion,
that I spend my spare time in the garden,
that I enthuse repeatedly about my wonderful granddaughter.

Thank you Lord that, now I'm retired,
I can get away with stuff
that would have been thought very odd
just ten years ago.
He, he, he!

And thank you God that nobody minds
that I fall asleep in the afternoon.

Brian Ford

## The woodland retreat

When I'm having a hard time finding space for God in my life, I go to 'the wood'.

This particular wood was the inspiration of my friend Vic who, for almost 20 years, cared for it as if it was his own back garden, until it was bought by the National Trust. But it's still the same wood with the same collection of seats that Vic constructed at special points along the many paths. It's a place where discerning dog-lovers walk their animals, and where just a few people (for not many know about this gem yet) come and wander amongst the tall beech trees or birch groves or beside sweet-chestnut stands.

This circular walk gives me the chance to meditate in different ways. I go for about two hours, stopping at various special points, and thanking God for all the stages of my life: toddlerhood, schooldays, student life, marriage and parenthood – and always the unknown future and what might be round the next bend of the path.

I've wandered round with various trouble spots of the world in my mind and prayers, stopping here for Ulster, there for Iraq, further along for South America …

Often it's the people in my life who take my attention at the resting points: family, church friends and (if I'm strong) those with whom I disagree. Now and then I give the time all to myself: my hopes and fears, my relationship with God and role in life.

And the wonderful thing about this sort of reflective walk is that anyone can do it, almost anywhere. It's repeatable even in suburbia; and if you don't have a wood nearby, there's probably a park, or a garden.

With age creeping on I've had to think creatively and prepare for when I can't get to the wood (or anywhere else). I've now latched onto the greatest possibility of all: using my imagination to create a walk for myself in familiar places that have meant so much to me: in the wood, round a Scottish bay, on a Welsh hillside, on the Otago Peninsula in New Zealand. I can recreate in my mind the sound of the wind, the smell of wet wood and sea air, the feel of bark or sand or rough boulders …

Paul Heppleston

## Saying grace

The deepest lessons
that a child learns
sink in without awareness:
so it was reflex
to say grace:
thank you for all your blessings, Lord:
Amen

My second age
left grace submerged
while I indulged
the luxury of outrage
believing it was courage:
considered all the world mismanaged
not myself estranged
and broken.

The rediscovery
amazes me.
'Thank you for the morning sky'
appeared when I was forty,
and day and daily
surges up again.

This morning
added a new note to the song:
suddenly from within
with neither will nor warning
something proclaiming:
'Thank you for sleep.'

Not like the prayer
that twists and tortures
me and my Maker,
sodden with my cares;
but simply being there,
happy to hear
the answering deep.

Roddy Cowie

# On becoming seventy: a personal liturgy

*Note: This is written for individual use but, with some minor amendments, could become a liturgy for worship with an elderly congregation.*

*Lord, you have been our dwelling-place in all generations ... from everlasting to everlasting you are God. (Psalm 90)*

Adoration:

From the beginning and for eternity, you are God.
In creation and in every living thing, you are God.
Through all history and in my daily life, you are God.
I worship and adore you.

You created me in your own image.
You offered me salvation through your Son.
Your Spirit renews and empowers me every day.
I worship and adore you.

You are my God.
You have led me with love through seventy years
and you will be with me forever.
My God, I worship and adore you.
Amen

Confession:

Loving God, as I look back upon my life,
I know that I must come to you in repentance.
For my story seems to tell of seventy years of sinning!
Not big ones, Lord, but so many silly little sins.

For the 'If only...' sins;
the 'Sorry, Lord, there I go again!' sins;
the 'You really can't blame me, Lord' sins:
Loving God, forgive me.

And for my septuagenarian sins ...
envy of those who had gifts that I lacked and longed for;
excuses I made for things left undone, and for things done but regretted;
fear, now, of what the future may hold for me:
Loving God, forgive me.

Loving God, Father of all, have mercy on me.
Jesus Christ, Son of God, have mercy on me.
Holy Spirit, Lord of Life, have mercy on me.

*The saying is sure and worthy of full acceptance, that Christ Jesus came into the world to save sinners. (1 Timothy 1:15)*

My sins are forgiven.
Thanks be to God.
Amen

**The Word** (Psalm 90:1–12)

**Reflection:**

Psalm 90, attributed to Moses, is a lament from a people wandering in the desert on their pilgrimage to the Promised Land. It becomes a reflection on the transient condition of human life and a reminder of God's involvement in their condition, as both Judge and Deliverer. Despite the sometimes melancholy words, neither defiance nor despair is expressed. In honesty, the Psalmist acknowledges guilt and that God's anger is warranted, but, in faith, he retains confidence in the God who remains their 'dwelling-place'. He concludes that everyone must be aware of their mortality and their accountability to God.

I have reached my biblical lifespan of seventy years – how will I use my bonus years?

In my 21st-century sophistication, can I recognise how small I am in the sight of God? And yet God loves me …

Am I seeking the wisdom of which the Psalmist speaks? Am I counting my days?

**Affirmation of faith:**

I believe in God the Father,
who has kept and guided me for seventy years.

I believe in Jesus Christ, his Son,
who has brought me into new life,
and whom I seek to follow faithfully.

I believe in the Holy Spirit,
who empowers and inspires me,
not least in the reading of these words.

**Song: 'Thanksgiving' (Tune: 'Moscow'):**

God, you have given to me
life that is full and free.
Praise to the Lord!
Family and friends to bless,
fair health and happiness;
so may I now confess:
Thanks be to God!

God, for this beauteous earth,
creation brought to birth:
Praise to the Lord!
All things that live display
your glory every day;
so with them all, I say:
Thanks be to God!

God, you have helped me see
life as it's meant to be.
Praise to the Lord!
Taught me to serve and care,
gifts that you gave to share;
that my life may declare:
Thanks be to God!

God, you will bring to birth
your Kingdom here on earth.
Praise to the Lord!
Meanwhile the Church must bring
Good News of Christ the King;
as we all join to sing:
Thanks be to God!

**Prayers for others (especially for older people in sorrow, need, anxiety, sickness):**

Loving God:
I pray for those who are sorrowful today.
For the bereaved: those who have lost their life partner, or friend or loved one.
For those who are sorrowful over past mistakes and missed opportunities in life.

I pray for those who are in need today.
For the hungry, the homeless and the oppressed around the world.

For those who cannot afford to eat properly or to heat their homes adequately.
For those who are lonely and need a friend.

I pray for those who are anxious today.
For those who worry about their health, or the health of a loved one.
For those who are concerned for the welfare of their families, perhaps far distant.
For those who feel helpless and useless, or unloved and unwanted.

I pray for those who are sick today in body, mind or spirit.
For those whose tired bodies are wearing out.
For those for whom illness makes living a constant struggle.
For the depressed, and for those who are gradually losing their grip on reality.

Loving God:
I pray that they all may find comfort and healing, courage and hope.
And to that end, I pray for wisdom for those in authority,
that they may honour older folk
and provide them with the services they need.

And I pray for the Church,
that Christians may be strengthened to maintain their wonderful ministry of caring
for their older sisters and brothers in Christ.
Loving God, I pray especially today for …

Lord, in your mercy, hear my prayers.
Amen

Blessing:

*Lord, you have been our dwelling-place in all generations … From everlasting to everlasting you are God. (Psalm 90:1–2)*

God, dwell in my heart today.
And may the blessing of God the Father, my Creator,
of Jesus Christ his Son, my Saviour and Friend,
and of the Holy Spirit, who comforts and empowers me,
remain with me all my days.
Amen

David Lemmon

## Growing old

To grow old is natural. We live in a finite world. Deterioration is part of the package which comes with life. When I was a baby I was able to put my big toe in my mouth. Development from that point is supposed to be a maturing process. But I can no longer put my big toe in my mouth. Body and mind wear out. We grow more and more limited in movement of bodies and the thinking of minds. It is a wearing process, sometimes no more than getting one day in after another, with nothing to show for the procession of days. My sister Margaret would say: 'God, are you not listening? Have you lost your hearing aid? It's time I was home.' But we are not called home at the time we would choose. We linger on, day after empty day. God's hearing aid proves to be elusive. Does it add up to anything? At different points of life we have been able to render forms of service for which we believed we were given life and to which we were called. But, thereafter … it is a drag-on. What sense does it make? The days creep slowly by adding up to …? Does anyone gain? Does God?

I suppose something positive may come out of the idea that it is 'payback' time. Children who have been reared with care and love get the chance to show sensitivity and compassion in their turn when the positions are reversed. That lightens old age. But old age is also unnatural, if we give what is natural a theological edge, is it not? All people are made in the likeness of God. Everyone has a place in God's purpose, forms of service to render, which is part of the response to the gift of life and of God's love, which is summed up in worship. What if all that becomes a blank for someone you love?

Dr Archie Craig and his wife retired to Doune. After a bit May lost the place; to the extent of asking on one occasion in her confused state: 'Does the name Archie Craig mean anything to you?' When a radio crew visited to interview him, Archie warned them: 'I have had to find a new way of loving.' He included May in the interview by saying something such as 'That is the way both of us think of the matter, isn't it, dear?' A simple affirmation on her part allowed her to feel included. His was a love which honoured fragility.

Shakespeare, in sonnet CXLVI, advises:
*'Within be fed, without be rich no more:*
*So shalt thou feed on death, that feeds on men,*
*And death once dead, there's no more dying then!'*

But that is advice for those who retain mental capacities to develop the resources of their inner life, when their legs can no longer carry them on life's journey, and they must put up at an inn.

Now that I am starting through my nineties I have to keep my own eyes open to signs that old age might be approaching.

My son, with sensitiveness to my thinking and wishes, refurbished my home to be manage-able, when I came to be less able to cope. It was a practical expression of my family's love. I suppose, though I am loth to admit it, that the same motivation was at work when I was asked to get rid of most of my books. 'We don't want to scratch our heads and wonder where to put them when you pop your clogs. You can put them where they can continue to be useful and used.' But how can a bird fly without its feathers?

I am still being encouraged to write articles, poems, hymns, especially by Wild Goose Publi-cations. But people are not, themselves, aware when they get 'past it'. Friends have assured me that they will count it part of our friendship to let me know when I am getting repetitive or dull and it is time to hang up my harp on a willow tree. Among the signs and portents of approaching old age I do not include the fact that I talk to myself – tell myself what I am doing and what I should be doing, assess what I have been doing. If you live on your own, who is there to talk to, unless others visit?

But there is now a kind of 'survival thankfulness' which did not mark earlier stages of my life. I wake in the morning to find that my body is still functioning, a cause for gratitude. At times of waking I reflect on the marvel of my body, all that blood continually pumped through it, lungs still functioning, one more day granted.

At this time of life there is also a thankfulness about simple things which occur in *'going in and out and finding pasture'*. What comes home to me with more force at this time of life is what my granny said when planning a journey: 'If we are weal (well) and spared … we will go and return.' I have known what it was to go into situations where a safe return could not nonchalantly be assumed. But the constant miracle of going somewhere and returning safely is something which I more vividly appreciate at this time of life – which says something about my stage and age.

Another thing which did not worry me earlier in life is cheek, jinky objects. I lay something down – a pen, spectacles, the box of stamps, let's say. My attention is diverted for a minute or two. When I look back they are gone. I check on my movements. Did I get up and move somewhere else, where I might have thoughtlessly left this or that? Nothing. In the end I go back to my seat. There the article is, exactly where it had been before, grinning as if to say, 'You thought you could always use me. But I got the better of you!' I have reason to resent these disappearances. Objects are meant to be inanimate. But am I the one who is getting to be inanimate?

Be sure to tell me if, one of these days, I start getting old. I won't know, myself!

Ian M. Fraser

# Travelling on

As I move towards my middle nineties I have to reckon with forms of dependency which accompany these later years.

There is physical dependency. Earlier this year I got a haemorrhage in my left eye. The Ophthalmology Unit doctor told me I must stop driving. So I am now more dependent on buses and I cadge lifts. Parts of my body show wear and tear, others get damaged in falls. I get more dependent on the marvelous National Health Service.

My main concern has to do with my thinking and writing. Iona Community member and economist Margaret Legum called these 'rigorous and accessible'. But for how long? I don't want to foist on people what may have lost its freshness and is merely repetitive. Yet I agree with Bishop Lesslie Newbigin, who was on my staff in Selly Oak colleges: 'You may retire at a certain time: but the day of your discharge is the day you die!' How can I give what may be still wanted of my life without making it a burden for others?

I have two safeguards.

One is that the books I have written have been asked for. It is other people who have approached me with the request that I write upon a certain subject, so that I don't depend on my own judgement. When that stops, I'll stop.

The other is the critical friendship of Wild Goose Publications. Some years ago editor Neil Paynter said to me, on their behalf, that they suspected that I had in old files and in my memory material that should get wider circulation. When I came across such writing would I send it in? They would stack it up and use it if and when and where it might be contributed to a book, and they might ask me to write on other allied subjects.

That provided two great gifts. One was an objective judgement on material – it was not left to me. The other comes into what I see as another aspect of 'critical friendship'. Whereas some other publishers might say, 'Ian might get a bit downhearted if we don't contrive to pick up some of his material', I can trust Wild Goose to say: 'You're losing it, Ian: time to shut up shop' – the advice of real friends can be trusted.

So I have a basis outside myself for knowing at what point mental alertness can no longer be counted on, as the years go by.

That points to the value of doing things as part of a community which can keep me right. Whenever my discharge comes, I hope that the prayer of John Wesley may have been mine – 'Let me be used for Thee or laid aside for Thee.'

Ian M. Fraser

## Day by day (for Nellie)

They say that age is a leveller.
It certainly is, as I observe
the ones who've learned to live just day by day
are shining in contentment.
They shed tears only for one another,
not themselves,
appreciate the smallest gesture:
a little cake, a cup of tea.
Their smile conveys a dignity of angels.
Their poverty's been made rich in giving
love and gratitude.
They know in wisdom
which cares are rightly theirs
and leave the rest alone.
The child heart is free
and heaven's already come to greet them
who have lived, and live still, trustingly.

Liz Gregory-Smith


## For Pat

She was 99 years young
99 years old

And your words, O God,
were often on her lips.
And your glory and wonder
was deep in her soul.

All those years and days
and she still told jokes
and she still asked questions.
She was full of stories,
full of psalms and songs.

And she knew
through all the light and dark
through her prayers and pain
through her courage and laughter

through the last confusing days of her journey
she knew
that she belonged to you, God,
and that her family and friends loved her
and she was going home.

Ruth Burgess


## The very best party

Celebrate
birth
life
death
resurrection.
Celebrate the whole of it.
Without question
this will be
the very best
party.

Pam Hathorn


## I've got to this length

So I've got to this length, Lord God.
As I look back over my life, I wonder what you make of it.
I know that the usual human measures for success don't apply –
on the cross Jesus was a failure to human eyes.
But you know better – and it is you I'll have to meet face to face
and give account.
I realise I'll get a shock when I see my life through your eyes,
but I also know the love of Jesus Christ for ordinary people
doing ordinary things to keep life going,
and his special compassion for those who have it rough and tough.
When my time comes I'll not rest my case.
I don't have a case.
I'll just rest my bones, trusting in him.

Ian M. Fraser

# Prayers for travelling

# What are you like, God?

What are you like, God?
You are here always.
Whether I talk to you
dance with you
blow you kisses
ignore you.
What are you like?
You are here always.

What am I like, God?
I'm a right mixture.
I can be gentle
and angry
and hurtful
and loving.
What am I like?
I'm a right mixture.

Keep me loving like you.
Do I want to pray that?
Do I want to change my behaviour?
You are not far away
and I'm lost without you.
Make me loving like you
and walk with me always.

Ruth Burgess

## I promise

Day by day
I will walk with you
I promise

Day by day
I will love my neighbour
I promise

Day by day
I will live in justice
I promise

Day by day
week by week
as the years pass by
you will keep me right.
(You will need to keep me right!)

Love you, God.
Thanks for your loving
always.

Ruth Burgess


## Today and tomorrow

Today
I love you, God.
I trust you.
I trust you with my dreams and questions.
Today I walk with you.

Tomorrow?
Who knows what comes tomorrow?
You may.
I don't.
Tomorrow I want to walk with you.

The more I walk with you
the more I seem to be full of questions.
The more the mystery deepens.

And that feels OK.
It doesn't stop me walking.

Some journey this,
some hope
some faith
some baptism.

Today
I love you, God.
Let's keep travelling.

Ruth Burgess


## Winter travelling

May the sharp frost
make us gasp for breath
and etch intricate patterns
of wonder and beauty
into the depths of who we are,
and who we might be.

Ruth Burgess


## Summertime

Flowers in the hedge
bees buzzing
warmth
wonder

short summer nights
long summer days

sunshine in the fields
sunshine in the city.

Summertime.

Thank you.

Ruth Burgess

## Will you?

Will you bless me, God?
Bless me with hope and wonder,
bless me with faith and questions,
bless me with strength and courage.
I want to walk with you all my days.
Bless me.

Will you bless me, God?
Bless me with a sense of justice,
bless me with tears and laughter,
bless me with friends and strangers.
I want to work with you all my days.
Bless me.

Will you bless me, God?
Bless me as I grow older,
bless me as my body grows tired,
bless me as death gets closer.
I want to be in love with you all my days.
Bless me.

Will you bless me, God?
Do I need to ask the question?
You have always blessed me,
in the light and in the darkness.
You have blessed me and cherished me
all my nights and days.

Ruth Burgess

# All your nights, all your days

May God
who is your maker and keeper
bless you today.

May Jesus
who understands tears and laughter
bless you today.

May the Holy Spirit
who sometimes shouts and sometimes whispers
bless you today.

May the angels
who are full of power and glory
bless you today.

May the little ones
who pull at your heart and your coat-sleeves
bless you today.

May the saints
who are more like you than you can ever imagine
bless you today

Today
tomorrow
all your nights
all your days
may you know God's blessing.
May you know you are deeply loved.

Ruth Burgess

## Time to go

Time to go now.
Time to find out what's round the corner.
Time to discover some of the answers to my questions.
Time to go.

Time to go now.
Time to share the love that's inside me.
Time to risk trusting Jesus.
Time to go.

Time to go now.
Time to listen to the Holy Spirit.
Time to walk with friends and strangers.
Time to go.

Hey God,
whatever time is
You made it –
nights of it,
days of it,
seconds and moments and hours and weeks and years of it.
You made me to dance and cry and smile and rejoice in it.

You call me now – ready or not!

Time to go.

Ruth Burgess

## Carpe diem

*Carpe diem*
go for it
pluck, seize, grab, enjoy
the moments of our nights and days

a ride on the Big Dipper
snowflakes falling
a multi-layered Knickerbocker Glory

the dance and crackle of burning wood
thick soup with dumplings
sunlight dancing on water
a Christmas carol
a small, squat, red-eyed solemn toad

a good film
a great concert
making blackberry and apple jelly
blowing airy dandelion clocks

a first breath
and a last one
a warm hug
shared laughter and tears

a project completed
a well-loved story
dragonflies and butterflies
bright stars and Venus in a December sky

*Carpe diem*
go on, go for it
pluck, seize, grab, enjoy, cherish
delight and dance in
the amazing moments
of our nights and days.

Ruth Burgess

## Sources and acknowledgements

'A nontraditional blessing' – by Sister Ruth Fox, OSB, Sacred Heart Monastery, Richardton, ND. Originally printed in *Living Faith*, 1989, as 'A mixed blessing'

'The blessing of a child (without baptism)' – by Joanna Anderson, from *The Pattern of Our Days: Liturgies and Resources for Worship*, Kathy Galloway, Wild Goose Publications, 1998

'May God, who laboured in love to create all life' – by Dorothy Brooker and others, from *Human Rites: Worship Resources for an Age of Change*, compiled by Hannah Ward and Jennifer Wild, Mowbray, 1995. Originally from *In other Words: Worship Resources for Women*, the Association of Anglican Women in the Diocese of Waipu, New Zealand, Napier, New Zealand

'An order of service for a baptism/naming/dedication of a child' – © Marjorie Dobson, first published in *Nothing Too Religious*, Marjorie Dobson and Andrew Pratt, Inspire 2008. Used by permission of Marjorie Dobson. (Book available through andrewpratt48@gmail.com)

'We were meeting in the long sitting-room ...' – From *Quaker Faith and Practice* (10.09), Quaker Books. Used by permission © The Religious Society of Friends (Quakers) in Britain

'In the dedication of this child you desire to give her/him fully to God ...' (Promises, from The Salvation Army) – © The Salvation Army. Used by permission of The Salvation Army

'Give us a swing, Jesus' – by Ruth Burgess, from *At Ground Level*, Ruth Burgess, Wild Goose Publications (out of print)

'Michael' – by Ruth Burgess, from *At Ground Level*, Ruth Burgess, Wild Goose Publications (out of print)

'Coming of age' – © Marjorie Dobson, first published in *Nothing Too Religious*, Marjorie Dobson and Andrew Pratt, Inspire 2008. Used by permission of Marjorie Dobson

'A wedding service/blessing of a partnership' – © Andrew Pratt, first published in *Nothing Too Religious*, Marjorie Dobson and Andrew Pratt, Inspire 2008. Used by permission of Andrew Pratt

'This is your day' – © Marjorie Dobson, first published in *Nothing Too Religious*, Marjorie Dobson and Andrew Pratt, Inspire 2008. Used by permission of Marjorie Dobson

'Love is the circle' – © Andrew Pratt, first published in *Nothing Too Religious*, Marjorie Dobson and Andrew Pratt, Inspire 2008. Used by permission of Andrew Pratt

'We meet at one point' – © Andrew Pratt, first published in *Nothing Too Religious*, Marjorie Dobson and Andrew Pratt, Inspire 2008. Used by permission of Andrew Pratt

# Contributors

*Joanna Anderson* is a member of the Iona Community and Island Centres Director for the Iona Community on Iona.

*Pete Anderson* is married to Joanna, is an Iona Community member, and has, as a consequence, been involved with the Community over the last 40 years or so, not least as a member of several Iona Resident groups.

*Stuart Barrie:* born in Govan, Glasgow 1944. Worked (from apprentice till retirement) as an engineer. Shop steward, poet, seeker after truths hidden in plain sight, perpetually dysfunctional human and don't care.

*John L. Bell* is a Resource Worker with the Iona Community, who lectures, preaches and conducts seminars across the denominations. He is a hymn writer, author and occasional broadcaster, but retains a primary passion for congregational song. John is based in Glasgow and works with his colleagues in the areas of music, worship and spirituality.

*Jan Berry* is a minister of the United Reformed Church working in theological education at Luther King House, where she teaches and supervises research in pastoral and practical theology, and liturgy and worship. She lives in south Manchester with her partner, Alma, plus two cats and a dog. She enjoys walking, meals with friends, and creating material for liturgy and worship. She has published her own collection of prayers, poems and hymns, *Naming God*, as well as material included in several anthologies.

*Lindsay Louise Biddle* is a writer and Presbyterian Church (USA) minister who lives in Glasgow and serves as chaplain of Affirmation Scotland and as a minister locum for the Church of Scotland.

*Andrew Bloomfield* leads his own life in Guelph, Ontario, Canada. As he cannot speak, he 'types to talk', and has published his autobiography, *Bridges Over Barriers in my Life with Autism* (2011), and about 150 poems.

*June Boyce-Tillman* is Professor of Applied Music at the University of Winchester, an Extraordinary Professor at North-West University South Africa and Convener of the Centre for the Arts as Well-being in Winchester. She is an honorary chaplain to Winchester Cathedral and an author, composer, performer, conductor and hymn writer. She was awarded an MBE for her services to music and education.

*Stuart Brock*: Born 1951. I was ordained in 1975 to URC ministry and served in Manchester and on Tyneside till 2004 when I took early retirement on health grounds. Since then I have occupied myself with a number of things, including writing a number of hymns and following interest in music of various kinds, especially folk music, as well as creative writing. I am married to Margaret, have four grown-up children and three grandchildren.

*Julia Brown* lives and works in Durham. She is married, with three grown-up children, the youngest being the two-year-old who inspired her poem here.

*Ruth Burgess* is a member of the Iona Community. She is busy being retired, writing, watching the antics of crows and jackdaws and growing fruit and vegetables. Ruth lives in Dunblane.

*John Butterfield* is a minister working in Central Scotland and a member of the Iona Community. He is married to Caroline and they have two grown-up children.

*David Coleman* job-shares URC ministry in Greenock with partner, Zam Walker. They are parents to Taliesin and Melangell. David is a digital artist with wide and uniquely long experience of multimedia in a worship context. He runs the Facebook page 'Lectionary clips and hymns'.

*Roddy Cowie* is Emeritus Professor of Psychology at Queen's University, Belfast, a lay reader in the Church of Ireland, and an associate member of the Iona Community.

*James Curry* is the Priest-in-Charge of two churches near Huddersfield.

*Liz Delafield:* I am a primary school teacher, living in Stockport, Greater Manchester with my husband Stewart and my children, Jennifer and Robert.

*Judy Dinnen:* Judy has worn many hats – wife, teacher, mother, social worker, poet and now priest and grandmother too. She is an associate member of the Iona Community and a lover of the island – the waves, rocks and the colours of the sky: a wonderful contrast to the green hills, apple trees and distant mountains of the Herefordshire countryside where she lives.

*Carol Dixon* was born in Alnwick, Northumberland and is a lay preacher in the United Reformed Church. Her hymns and prayers have been published in *All Year Round, Songs for the New Millennium, Worship Live*, the Church of Scotland hymnbook (CH4) and on HymnQuest. She is a wife, mother and grandmother.

*Marjorie Dobson* is a Methodist Local Preacher and writer of hymns, prayers, poetry and drama for worship. She had a solo collection of work published in 2004 and has co-authored two further collections with Andrew Pratt, published in 2006 and 2008.

*Brid Fitzpatrick* is a member of the Catholic Women's Network, and for thirty years she has been interested in language and how the way we use it shapes the way we understand the world, ourselves and God.

*Brian Ford:* I was a biology teacher for the whole of my working life. I retired seven years ago and since then there have been quite a few changes in my life.

*Andrew Foster* is an engineer living in Ontario, Canada, an associate of the Iona Community, an elder in the Presbyterian Church in Canada, a frequent visitor to Iona, and a contributor to some of Ruth Burgess's previous books.

*Sally Foster-Fulton* is the associate minister at Dunblane Cathedral and the Convener of the Church of Scotland's Church and Society Council. Sally is originally from South Carolina, is married to Stuart; they have two beautifully creative and unique daughters, Alex and Gracie. She is the author of *Hope Was Heard Singing* (Wild Goose Publications).

*Ian M. Fraser* has been a pastor-labourer in heavy industry, a parish minister, Warden of Scottish Churches House, an Executive Secretary of the World Council of Churches, and Dean and Head of the Department of Mission at Selly Oak Colleges, Birmingham. He is the author of numerous books, including *Strange Fire*, *The Way Ahead*, *A Storehouse of Kingdom Things* and *Reinventing Theology* (Wild Goose). Ian is one of the original members of the Iona Community who helped George MacLeod to rebuild 'the common life' and the Abbey buildings on the isle of Iona. Throughout his life Ian has travelled the world, alone and with his wife, Margaret, visiting basic Christian communities. He has walked alongside slum dwellers in India and Haiti; Nicaraguan and Cuban revolutionaries; priests, nuns and catechists facing arrest and/or death in Central and South America; and small farming and fishing communities in the Philippines.

*Linda Fraser:* I am a 66-year-old pensioner. I live alone with my cat Bernie, and enjoy writing short poems.

*Alma Fritchley:* Alma has been a fiction writer over the years and has had several novels published. She is a member of Central URC/Baptist Church in Manchester and is currently studying for a BA in contextual theology at Luther King House. She lives with her civil partner, Jan.

*Terry Garley:* An Anglican married to a Methodist, a former foreign language teacher and County Ecumenical Officer (for Derbyshire & Nottinghamshire 1990-2000 and for Lancashire 2000-2008). Now retired, I continue to write prayers for the parish church and pieces for the local Methodist and URC news. This particular prayer was written for our Ruby Anniversary in 2006.

*Mark Godin and Alana Vincent* reside in the Northwest of England. Alana is Lecturer in Jewish Studies at the University of Chester; Mark is a minister of the Presbyterian Church in Canada but is currently serving St Andrew's Handbridge United Reform Church. They have both received PhDs from the University of Glasgow's Centre for Literature, Theology and the Arts, and have each published widely on religion, art and Continental philosophy.

*Kes Grant:* I am an unorthodox Church of England priest. Previously I was a hospital chaplain and now work as a full-time school chaplain.

*Christine Green* is a member of the Iona Community living in Cumbria. She is a legal secretary, and a voluntary befriender with SANDS (Stillbirth And Neonatal Death Society).

*Liz Gregory-Smith* lives on the edge of Durham City with her husband, David. Liz is an Anglican Reader with permission to officiate in the local Anglican church.

*David Hamflett* is a Methodist minister and a Friend of the Iona Community working in the north of England, who has a special interest in compiling and composing liturgies. He sings traditional folk songs and plays the guitar and the bodhrán and has recently taken up the Irish bouzouki.

*Mary Hanrahan:* I am currently enjoying my retirement, learning new skills in craft and writing groups and rediscovering wonder by spending time with my grandson, Tom. I am an active member in my parish community of St Paul the Apostle, Shettleston and a regular poet at Lentfest, our Archdiocesan celebration of the arts.

*Catherine Harkin:* I am a GP and writer living and working in Edinburgh.

*John Harvey* is a retired Church of Scotland parish minister and a member of the Iona Community. With his wife, Molly, he has been involved recently in supporting the work of the Poverty Truth Commission in Glasgow and west central Scotland.

*Ruth Harvey* lives and works in Cumbria where she is a church-based mediator and ecumenical officer. She is a Quaker, Presbyterian and member of the Iona Community.

*Pam Hathorn:* Retired teacher who enjoys sharing her time with many people and is embracing new areas of learning and spiritual life.

*Paul Heppleston* is a musician and writer currently living on the edge of the Peak District. He also leads small-group holidays to remote parts of Britain with www.journeying.co.uk

*Karen Kinloch* was born in 1969 with Down's Syndrome and is now severely disabled with arthritis but still manages to enjoy life, swimming at least 1 mile every week and playing both piano and organ. She brings lots of joy to her extended family and many friends, including those on the Internet.

*Sandra Kramer* has lived at Samye Ling Tibetan Centre and the Findhorn Community, and now works for the Iona Community at Wild Goose Publications.

*David Lemmon* is a retired youth worker and youth work trainer, living in Beckenham, Kent. He is a Methodist Local Preacher and a Friend of the Iona Community.

*Pat Livingstone* is a composer and music educator and a member of the Iona Community. She has recently received an MMus in Composing for film and TV.

*Campbell Macaulay* (1955–2000) was a committed socialist who gave his time freely to the grassroots projects he believed in, such as the Benwell Law Centre and the Cruddas Park Tenants Association. A gifted artist, he was also generous in using his talents for projects which his wife believed in, among other things helping to produce a guide for a women's tour of Durham Cathedral and designing a very striking logo for the North East Ecumenical Women's Group.

Until recently *Glendon Macaulay* was a Church of Scotland minister in Falkirk where he took particular interest in working (often ecumenically) with congregations to encourage and develop innovative and creative worship styles. He is the author of *Dirt, Mess and Danger* (Wild Goose Publications).

*Janet MacDonald* is a member of the Iona Community living and working in Glasgow.

*June McAllister* lives a peaceful and solitary life in County Galway with dogs and hens, and grows organic vegetables. She is involved in local rural concerns, is a Cancer Care volunteer, a prison chaplaincy volunteer, spiritual guide and counsellor.

*Kate McIlhagga* was a minister and a member of the Iona Community until her death in 2002. Her intimate, insightful prayers and poems are loved and used by people far and wide for both personal and group prayer and reflection.

*Colin McIntosh* was minister at Dunblane Cathedral for 25 years and retired in August 2013. Previously he was minister of St John's-Renfield Church in Glasgow.

*David McNeish* worked as a hospital doctor, worship musician and campaigner for the Citizens Advice Bureau, before admitting defeat and training as a Church of Scotland minister. A member of the Iona Community, he lives in South Queensferry with his wife Sally and three children.

*Ashley-Anne Masters* is ordained in the Presbyterian Church (USA) and is a pastor, author and hospital chaplain in Chicago, IL. She is author of *Holding Hope: Grieving Pregnancy Loss During Advent* (Church Health Center) and co-author of *Bless Her Heart: Life as a Young Clergywoman* (Chalice Press). She blogs at revaam.org.

*Carolyn Morris:* Berkshire ex-teacher, now a part-time book creator, crafter, writer and, of necessity, house decorator.

*Isabel Morrison* studied music at the Royal Scottish Academy of Music and Drama in Glasgow. She has been teaching piano, clarinet and singing in Northumberland for over 35 years and has played the organ at St Mark's URC in Amble for almost 30 years. She has always enjoyed composing and arranging music and particularly enjoys the challenge of writing to specific criteria.

*Katie Munnik* is a Canadian writer living in Edinburgh with her husband and three growing children. She works as Associate for Children and Families at Canongate Kirk and writes a weekly online column called 'The Messy Table' for the *Presbyterian Record*. You can find Katie on twitter @messy_table.

*Katy Owen:* Volunteered to teach English to students at the Grameen Caledonian Nursing College in Dhaka, Bangladesh. Working in the community with Woman's Aid, helping to run a foot clinic for homeless folk in Glasgow, and visiting care homes with a singing group and reminiscence boxes.

*Sarah Pascoe:* ex-nurse, mother and grandmother, who loves living beside the sea.

*Neil Paynter* is an editor, author and late-night piano player.

*Chris Polhill* is a member of the Iona Community and one of the first women priests in the Church of England. She has contributed to a number of Wild Goose books and is the author of *Eggs and Ashes* (with Ruth Burgess), *A Pilgrim's Guide to Iona Abbey* and *A Heart for Creation*. She and her husband, John, run the Reflection Gardens, which highlights the Christian spiritual journey and environmental issues.

*John Polhill* is a retired systems designer and Environmental Officer for the Diocese of Lichfield.

*Travis Poling* writes poetry and teaches English in Richmond, Indiana. He curates worship at the Richmond Church of the Brethren.

*Andrew Pratt* is a Methodist minister and hymn writer who has taught Pastoral and Practical Theology to people preparing for ministry at Luther King House in Manchester.

*Karen Reeves* serves as a Pioneer Minister in Coventry and enjoys the challenge of membership in the Iona Community.

*Katherine Rennie* is a member of the Iona Community and a local preacher with the Methodist Church.

*David Rhodes,* an Iona associate, writes on social justice and the love of God. His most recent book, *Faith in Dark Places* (SPCK), challenges the Church to work for a more just and equitable society.

*Blair Robertson* is a minister of the Church of Scotland. Since 2006 he has coordinated the work of Affirmation Scotland: a network of LGBT Christians, friends and supporters in the Church. He is Head of Healthcare Chaplaincy and Spiritual Care for NHS Greater Glasgow and Clyde.

*Anne Seymour*: I went to Nigeria as a medic in 1961 and was still there in 1967 when the civil war started. Worked through the war and was deported after it. Became consultant in A&E in South Tyneside till 1989, when I went to Cameroon for seven years. Retired in 1996. Now secretary to an ecumenical charity supporting refugees and asylum seekers.

*Norman Shanks* is a retired Church of Scotland minister and a former Leader of the Iona Community.

*Annie Sharples* lives in Wrexham with her family and two dogs. She enjoys reading and attending music concerts.

*Mary Sharples* lives in Wrexham with her family and two dogs. She enjoys drawing and reading.

*Richard Sharples* is a Methodist minister trying to live a simple life and explore 'new ways to touch the hearts of all'. He is married to Biddy and with their three daughters lives in Wrexham, North Wales.

*Thom M. Shuman,* a poet and pastor, has contributed to a number of Wild Goose books, and is the author of *The Jesse Tree* and *Gobsmacked* (Wild Goose).

*Muriel Snell* is a retired civil servant living in Failsworth near Manchester.

*Simon Taylor* is a Baptist minister and university chaplain in Exeter. His daughter Kira, now 15, loves to write and hopes herself to be an author.

*Fiona van Wissen:* I spent eight winters living in Italy with the L'Arche community near Rome. I am currently working for the Presbyterian Church in Canada planning youth and adult programmes at Crieff Hills Retreat Centre near Guelph, Ontario.

*Zam Walker* is a minister of the United Reformed Church in Greenock who job-shares ministry and childcare with her husband, David Coleman. Both are members of the Iona Community. Particular passions are body theology and celebration of diversity.

*Pat Welburn:* For 12 years I was principal officer in a Christian adoption agency.

*Wellspring:* Kathryn Turner and Catherine McElhinney have worked together as Wellspring for over 20 years. During this time they have created a wide range of liturgy and spirituality resources which have been published in print form and through their website: www.wellsprings.org.uk

*Jean Williams* is a member of the Iona Community. She has conducted workshops on 'Celtic' spirituality in Scotland and Canada.

*Sheila Woodcock* is a member of the Iona Community, a retired pharmacist and mother of two daughters. For three years she was a resident member of staff on Iona.

*Stephen Wright* is an author and poet working as a spiritual director for a charity based in Cumbria (www.sacredspace.org.uk).

# Index of authors

# Wild Goose Publications is part of the Iona Community:

- An ecumenical movement of men and women from different walks of life and different traditions in the Christian church
- Committed to the gospel of Jesus Christ, and to following where that leads, even into the unknown
- Engaged together, and with people of goodwill across the world, in acting, reflecting and praying for justice, peace and the integrity of creation
- Convinced that the inclusive community we seek must be embodied in the community we practise

Together with our staff, we are responsible for:

- Our islands residential centres of Iona Abbey, the MacLeod Centre on Iona, and Camas Adventure Centre on the Ross of Mull

*and in Glasgow:*

- The administration of the Community
- Our work with young people
- Our publishing house, Wild Goose Publications
- Our association in the revitalising of worship with the Wild Goose Resource Group

The Iona Community was founded in Glasgow in 1938 by George MacLeod, minister, visionary and prophetic witness for peace, in the context of the poverty and despair of the Depression. Its original task of rebuilding the monastic ruins of Iona Abbey became a sign of hopeful rebuilding of community in Scotland and beyond. Today, we are about 250 Members, mostly in Britain, and 1500 Associate Members, with 1400 Friends worldwide. Together and apart, 'we follow the light we have, and pray for more light'.

For information on the Iona Community contact:
The Iona Community, Fourth Floor, Savoy House, 140 Sauchiehall Street,
Glasgow G2 3DH, UK. Phone: 0141 332 6343
e-mail: admin@iona.org.uk; web: www.iona.org.uk

For enquiries about visiting Iona, please contact:
Iona Abbey, Isle of Iona, Argyll PA76 6SN, UK. Phone: 01681 700404
e-mail: ionacomm@iona.org.uk